W9-CEK-250

Contents

Introduction

Welcome to the wonderful world of food. We all need it, we all eat it and now you're going to find out how to cook it.

It would be easy never to prepare a meal again – supermarkets are packed full with ready-made meals, but where's the fun in that? It's true you'll have to find time to buy all the ingredients and get everything ready, as well as doing the actual cooking, but the thrill of serving and eating something you have made with your own clean hands is amazing.

This book is split into sections. The first part is the bossy bit, which tells you what to do, and what not to do, to be safe in the kitchen. Then there's lots of information about equipment and, at the end of the book, there is a glossary to explain words used in the recipes that you might not understand. Choosing what to cook is exciting as there are plenty of recipes to pick from. Some dishes are simple and easier to cook – these are marked with one 🍴 and are a good place to start if you haven't done any cooking before. Once you have cooked a few of the simple recipes, you can try some of the slightly trickier recipes that have two 🍴. There are also recipes that are more difficult to cook, they have three 🍴.

The basic cooking techniques have also been included, so you will learn a lot of useful skills as you make each different recipe. These will certainly be valuable one day when you have to cook for yourself. You'll probably be cooking for your friends too, once they taste the amazing dishes you have cooked.

As well as stacks of tasty snacks and savoury meals, there are plenty of party dishes, delicious desserts and drinks, cakes and other bakes to choose from – so put on your apron, get cooking and have a great time!

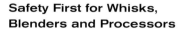

Be Safe in the Kitchen

◆ Before you start, check with an adult that it is okay to cook. Ask for help if you need it.

◆ Shut pets out of the kitchen when you are cooking. Not only is cat hair in the gravy horrid and unhealthy, but you could also trip over a small and scurrying creature. This rule may also apply to younger brothers and sisters.

◆ If you have long hair, tie it back.

◆ Make sure you turn all pan handles to the sides of the stove when they're on the hob (stovetop). This will stop you knocking the pan over or catching yourself on the handle. It will also prevent the handle from scorching or melting.

◆ Never touch electrical equipment, plugs, sockets or switches when your hands are wet. You might get an electric shock.

◆ Take care when using sharp knives. Chop on a chopping board and point the knife downwards, keeping your fingers out of the way.

◆ Stand away from frying food or boiling water. Always ask an adult to help with these stages.

◆ Never leave hot oil unattended.

Right: When cutting things, always use a chopping board and keep your fingers away from the knife blade.

◆ If you spill anything on the floor while you are cooking, always wipe it up straight away. If you leave it, you might forget it's there and slip later.

◆ It's a good idea to have a heatproof mat or a metal stand handy on the table to put hot pans on to.

◆ Use proper oven gloves and potholders to lift hot dishes – a dishtowel trailing across the hob (stovetop) can easily catch fire.

◆ A large pan or casserole can be very heavy when it is full. If you are not sure that you can lift it, ask an adult to help.

◆ Don't wander off leaving pans to boil dry or, even worse, catch fire. If you have to go out of the kitchen, turn the heat off first.

Safety First for Whisks, Blenders and Processors

◆ Never put your hand in a blender or food processor to move something while it is plugged in.

◆ Keep small fingers away from whisks while they are whizzing around.

◆ Treat electrical equipment very carefully and always unplug blenders and processors before you empty the goblet. Ask an adult to help you to fit special blades or attachments.

Safety First for Ovens and Hobs/Stovetops

◆ When the oven is working, the door can become very hot and this can be dangerous. If your oven is new, it probably has a stay-cool door, which is much safer.

◆ Don't stand dishes on the oven door as it is not designed to take the weight and is unstable.

◆ Don't turn the heat under a pan too high to speed things up, because not only could you spoil the dish you're cooking, but you may also scorch the pan, melt the handle or cause everything to boil over.

Safety First for Microwave Ovens

◆ Never put any foil, metal dishes or pans, or plates with metallic edges, such as a silver line on the rim, in microwave ovens. Check with an adult that dishes are microwave-safe before you use them.

◆ Follow the recipe instructions carefully. The standing time mentioned at the end of microwave recipes is part of the cooking, so don't be tempted to skip it.

◆ Be very careful when lifting bowls of liquid ingredients out of the microwave because they continue to cook and can bubble up over the top of the bowl.

Index

Getting Started

The very first thing you must always do before you start to cook your favourite dish is to get permission from an adult. It is also sensible to show them the recipe.

The recipes in this book show you, in detailed stages, what you should be doing at each step of the cooking. Just take a look at the step-by-step pictures and the recipe method and follow them.

So, when you have read through the rest of the information in this introduction, off you go. Good luck and have fun!

Below: Once you've read the recipe and washed your hands, you should always put on an apron so that you don't dirty your clothes.

First Things First

You've chosen your recipe and bought the ingredients, but there are a few simple things to do before you actually start to cook. If there is anything you don't understand, ask an adult to explain it to you.

◆ Read through the recipe very carefully, from start to finish, so you have a clear idea of what you are about to be doing and in what order.

◆ Wash and dry your hands. If your hair is long, tie it back. Put on an apron to protect your clothes – plastic ones are best.

◆ Make sure the kitchen surfaces are clean and tidy and you have plenty of space in which to work.

◆ Get all the ingredients you will need ready and measured.

Above: When in doubt, ask an adult for a helping hand. As you do more cooking, you will become more of an expert.

Why Things go Wrong

If you find that things are not turning out as they should, then make sure you are following this list of handy tips.

◆ Don't rush.

◆ Do read the recipe through before you start, and follow the instructions and pictures closely.

◆ Do weigh and measure the ingredients carefully.

◆ Don't have any interruptions or distractions while you are in the kitchen, as this can cause you to forget where you are in the recipe, and leave something out.

◆ If you are cooking something in the oven, don't keep opening the oven door as this will cause the temperature to drop.

◆ Do make sure you cook things for the proper length of time.

◆ If you don't understand a cooking term, check the glossary in this book or ask an adult.

Oiling This term may mean the same as greasing (see above) and is also used for brushing oil on a griddle or omelette pan before cooking.

Par-boil To start cooking food, such as potatoes, in boiling water before moving on to the next stage of the cooking process, such as roasting. Par-boiling is a good way to speed up the roasting time.

Pipe To squeeze a mixture out of a bag through a nozzle to make a particular shape. This technique is used for icing (frosting) and for some cake and biscuit (cookie) doughs. The final shape depends on the size and shape of nozzle. Piping requires a steady hand.

Process Whizzing ingredients together in a food processor or blender to mix them thoroughly or to blend them smoothly, as with soup.

Prove Once bread dough has been kneaded for 5 minutes and is smooth and elastic, it is covered and left somewhere warm to double in size. This is called proving the dough.

Purée This French word describes a smooth, creamy, almost liquid food. Vegetables are often puréed for soup either by processing them in a blender or food processor, or by pressing them through a sieve with the back of a wooden spoon. Soft raw fruit, such as strawberries, or cooked fruit, such as plums, may also be turned into a purée for desserts and sauces.

Roll out Pastry dough is rolled with a rolling pin to make a smooth, flat sheet. Remember to sprinkle a little flour on the work surface first to stop the dough from sticking. Use a heavy rolling pin and let it do the work – don't press down, just guide it across the dough. Always roll in one direction only, turning the dough from time to time, adding more flour to stop it from sticking to the work surface.

Rub in This technique is one of the first steps in making pastry and some other doughs. Butter or other fat, cut into small pieces, is added to flour and then the two are worked together by rubbing them with the tips of your fingers. Once combined, the mixture looks like breadcrumbs. It is important to keep the mixture as cool as possible, so a good alternative to fingertips is a pastry blender, a curved metal tool with a handle.

Season Usually, this simply means to add salt and pepper to a dish, but can also include other ingredients, such as grated nutmeg, curry powder or vinegar. Seasoning adds flavour to the dish. Tasting a spoonful of the dish is the best way to judge whether you have added enough seasoning.

Shallow Fry To cook food in a thin layer of oil, so it browns and crisps on the outside..

Sift Shaking ingredients such as flour or icing (confectioners') sugar through a fine strainer not only gets rid of any lumps, but also helps to add air when mixing cakes or pastry.

Simmer To cook food slowly and gently in liquid, such as stock or a sauce. Once the liquid has come to the boil, turn down the heat so that the surface bubbles very gently and only occasionally.

Snipping Using kitchen scissors to cut things in small pieces, rather than chopping them. This is a good way to cut up bacon, herbs and dried fruit.

Stir-fry This quick and easy cooking technique was invented in China and is now popular throughout the world. The ingredients are finely chopped or thinly sliced and then fried over a high heat, usually in a wok, while they are constantly stirred and tossed. As you need only a little amount of oil, this is more healthy than shallow frying.

Stock When vegetable trimmings and bones boil in water, their flavour is picked up and the water turns to stock. Stock cubes can be bought at most supermarkets and come in a variety of flavours.

Strain This is a method of filtering a liquid. It is often used when making sauces to remove flavouring ingredients, such as onion and spices, that are no longer required.

Thicken Sauces that are thin and too watery are given more body when a thickening agent such as cornflour (corn starch) is added to the sauce.

Whisk Ingredients such as double (heavy) cream, egg whites and sponge cake mixtures are beaten hard with a whisk so that they become light and airy.

Weighing and Measuring

The ingredients in this book are measured using grams (g) and millilitres (ml), known as metric measures. They are also measured in ounces (oz), fluid ounces (fl oz) and pints, which are known as imperial measures. You will also find cup measurements. It is very important that you choose only one type of measurement. Be careful not to mix the units – use either grams and millilitres or ounces and pints. Similarly, keep to cup measurements if that's what you prefer. However, teaspoons and tablespoons are the same in all systems.

Measuring Cups, Spoons and Jugs

Cup measurements given in recipes are not just any old cup, but a standard measuring cup. Sets of measuring cups usually include four sizes: ¼, ⅓, ½ and 1 cup.

You will also see tsp for teaspoon and tbsp for tablespoon and, again, these are special measuring spoons. Sets of spoons usually have four or five different sizes: 1.5ml/¼ tsp, 2.5ml/½ tsp, 5ml/1 tsp, 15ml/1 tbsp. Sometimes they also include a 10ml/1 dessert spoon and 0.6ml/⅛ tsp, but these measurements are not used in this book. Just to confuse everybody, Australian tablespoons are slightly bigger – 20ml. In some countries, such as Britain, where people don't generally use measuring cups for dry or liquid ingredients, they use a measuring jug. These special jugs are made of glass or a see-through plastic and they usually allow you to measure quantities up to 600ml/20fl oz. Most measuring jugs also have a graded scale printed on the side of the jug so that you can measure smaller amounts as well.

Left: Kitchen scales are useful for measuring dry ingredients.

Above: When you are adding ingredients, ensure that you measure them accurately.

Kitchen Scales

Modern kitchen scales, whether spring or electronic, usually measure in both metric (grams) and imperial (ounces) units. Electronic scales display the weight in a panel and are easy to use. Spring scales have a dial and the best way to read it is to move your head so that your eyes are level with the pointer. Always check that the dial is on zero before you start to measure your ingredients.

How to Measure

When using cups and spoons to measure dry ingredients, the ingredient should be level, not heaped. The best way to do this is to scoop up and then scrape gently across the top of the cup or spoon with the blunt side of the blade of a knife. Of course, you don't need to do this with liquids as they don't heap up in the first place. You should always check the outside of the measuring cup, as the top measurement for each size is usually marked just below the rim so that the liquid doesn't overflow.

Glossary

Bake This is a method of cooking in the dry heat of the oven – you don't add fat, stock or other liquids. Cakes, biscuits (cookies), bread and pies are typical baked dishes.

Beat This is an energetic way of mixing ingredients together. It is also a way of making them light and airy, such as when butter and sugar are beaten together when you are making a cake. Beating is usually done with a wooden spoon, but eggs are lightly beaten together with a fork.

Bind When liquid, such as water, milk or beaten egg, is added to dry ingredients, it makes them stick together or bind. This word is most often used in recipes for making dough, such as pastry.

Boil A liquid is boiling when the edges are rolling over and large bubbles appear on the surface.

Brown Meat and vegetables are often browned at the beginning of a recipe to give them an even colour. The food is usually cooked in hot fat in a pan and turned over frequently.

Core To cut out the tough central part and seeds of a fruit. This is easily done with an apple corer. Push the corer into the fruit over the stalk, and twist. When you pull the corer out, the core should come out too.

Cream Sometimes recipes tell you to cream ingredients, usually butter or margarine and sugar, together. This just means beating them hard to mix well and make them light and creamy in texture.

Dice To cut an ingredient, such as carrots or butter, into small cubes.

Drain To pour away the liquid, very often boiling water, that you have used for cooking an ingredient, such as potatoes. A colander is usually the most useful tool for doing this. Stand the colander in the sink and pour the contents of the pan into it, taking care not to splash yourself. The water will go out of the holes and down the drain, while your cooked vegetables or pasta will remain in the colander.

Dry ingredients This term is most often used in recipes for cakes, biscuits (cookies) and bread. Dry ingredients, which might include flour, sugar and raisins, are often mixed first, then wet ingredients, such as milk and eggs, are mixed together before the whole lot are combined.

Glaze Brushing pastry or bread with egg or milk will make it shiny and look more attractive.

Grease Often baking sheets, cake tins (pans) and some other dishes need a thin coating of butter, margarine or vegetable oil to prevent dough or cake mixture from sticking to them. Oiling is easiest because you can brush the oil evenly over the surface with a pastry brush. Rub on butter or margarine with a piece of greaseproof (waxed) paper.

Knead Pressing, stretching and turning a mixture or dough with your hands helps to make it smooth and, in the case of bread dough, stretchy. Pastry and scones, however, should be kneaded very lightly or you will knock out all the air and they will become heavy and hard.

Level Cake recipes often tell you to level the surface of the mixture after you have spooned it into the tin (pan). This helps to make sure that the cake cooks evenly and that it looks nice. Use a palette knife or metal spatula to spread the mixture.

Lukewarm This term is used when a just-warm liquid is to be added to dry ingredients. It should feel neither hot nor cold.

Marinate This is a way of adding flavour to savoury ingredients, such as meat, fish or vegetables. The food is left to steep in a mixture of flavouring ingredients – a marinade – that might include lemon juice, vinegar, herbs or spices. Marinating can also help to make meat more tender.

Mash Boiled potatoes are the most popular vegetable for mashing, although many other ingredients, such as bananas, can also be reduced to a smooth texture by bashing them. Butter, oil, milk and other liquids are sometimes added before mashing for extra creaminess and lightness. A potato masher is ideal for vegetables, such as swede (rutabaga), and you can also use a potato ricer or food mill. A fork is harder work, but still effective. Never try to mash cooked vegetables in a food processor – it makes them too smooth and sticky.

Kitchen Tools

There are a lot of weird and wonderful things in kitchen cupboards and drawers. Here's a guide to help you find out what they are.

Knives

These must be used very carefully. Try not to be distracted when chopping or cutting ingredients. Always pick the right size knife for the right job: don't use a huge bread knife to peel an apple. You will need five basic knives to do most jobs in this book: a paring knife, with a 7.5cm/3in blade, for peeling and trimming fruit and vegetables; a cook's knife, with a 15cm/6in blade, for general slicing; a chopping knife, with a 20cm/8in blade, for chopping and slicing; a bread knife, with a 25cm/10in serrated-edge blade, for cutting bread; and a palette knife, with a long, flexible blade, for lifting and spreading. Knives become blunt after a while and should be sharpened, using a special knife-sharpening gadget.

Below: A cook's knife (left) and a paring knife

Kitchen Scissors

Use for cutting things like bacon, or snipping fresh herbs.

Above: Kitchen scissors

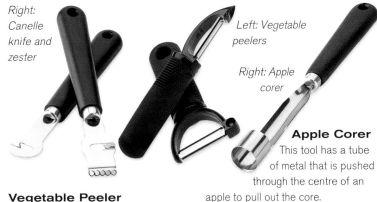

Right: Canelle knife and zester

Left: Vegetable peelers

Right: Apple corer

Vegetable Peeler

Some peelers have fixed blades with wooden handles and others have a blade that moves. Those with moving blades make peeling easier. Vegetable peelers can also be used to make elegant slices of Parmesan cheese to top cooked dishes such as pastas.

Zester

This is a small tool with five tiny round blades at the end. When it is dragged across citrus fruits, such as oranges or lemons, it removes long thin shreds of the rind. These can be used either in a recipe or to garnish a salad.

Canelle Knife

This is just like a zester, but it cuts a thicker strip of rind.

Can Opener

The two "arms" of the can opener are squeezed together, so the blades pierce the can. When you turn the handle round and round, the top of the can will come off. Be careful not to spill any of the can's contents.

Apple Corer

This tool has a tube of metal that is pushed through the centre of an apple to pull out the core.

Lemon Squeezer

This handy tool is used to extract juice from citrus fruits. Use by pressing the cut side of a halved citrus fruit over the central "spike". The juice will then run down and collect in the bottom half or bowl part of the squeezer.

Left: Metal lemon squeezer

Garlic Press

Crushed garlic has a stronger flavour than chopped garlic. The press will squash the garlic cloves through small holes ready for cooking.

Skewers

Metal or wooden ones can be used to spear ingredients for kebabs. To prevent wooden skewers from burning, you should soak them in water for about 30 minutes before use. Metal skewers can also be used to push into cakes to test if they are cooked – the skewer comes out clean when the cake is cooked.

Lemon Meringue Cakes

This is a much more exciting version of rather boring fairy cakes – soft lemon sponge cakes are topped with crisp meringue.

You will need

115g/4oz/½ cup margarine
200g/7oz/scant 1 cup caster (superfine) sugar
2 eggs
115g/4oz/1 cup self-raising (self-rising) flour
5ml/1 tsp baking powder
grated rind of 2 lemons
30ml/2 tbsp lemon juice
2 egg whites

Makes 18 🍰🍰🍰

3 Whisk the egg whites in a clean, grease-free bowl, until they stand in soft peaks. Stir in the remaining caster sugar and lemon rind.

4 Put a spoonful of the meringue mixture on each cake. Cook for 20–25 minutes, until the meringue is crisp and brown. Serve hot or cold.

1 Preheat the oven to 190°C/375°F/ Gas 5. Beat the margarine until soft. Add 115g/4oz/½ cup of the sugar and continue to beat until the mixture is smooth and creamy.

2 Beat in the eggs, flour, baking powder, half the lemon rind and all the lemon juice. Stand 18 paper cases in two bun tins (muffin pans), and share the mixture among them.

Wooden Spoon

These come in various lengths. It is better to use shorter ones for beating cake mixtures and for stirring melted chocolate, but wooden spoons with longer handles are best for cooking on the hob, because your hand is further from the heat.

Wooden Spatulas

A wooden spatula is like a wooden spoon but the end is flattened instead of round. Large flat spatulas are ideal for making scrambled eggs, while one with holes can be used to beat eggs and mix sauces.

Basting Spoon

This is a large metal spoon that is used to pour sauce or meat juices over baked dishes, such as roasts. Basting meat while it cooks will ensure that it is moist and tender.

Slotted Spoons

These come in various shapes and sizes, and are excellent for lifting and draining fried food. Be careful not to spill any hot oil when draining food.

Ladle

A large, deep spoon, used mainly for serving soup. Ladles can also be used to dish up savoury stews and desserts such as fruit salad.

Rubber Spatula

This is just like a wooden spatula but it has a flexible rubber blade. It is especially good for scraping the mixture or batter from mixing bowls.

Fish/Egg Slices

These are used to lift and turn burgers, fish, or fried eggs. Always use special plastic fish or egg slices on non-stick pans as this will protect the suface of the pan and prevent it from getting ruined.

Tongs

Used for turning things over, they allow you to grip meat and fish easily. You can also buy special outdoor tongs to use when cooking on a barbecue.

Sieves

These come in various sizes. Smaller ones are ideal for sifting icing sugar (confectioners' sugar) over cakes and desserts, and larger ones can be used for sifting dry ingredients and for draining vegetables.

Balloon Whisk

Whisks are best used to add air to cream or eggs to make them light. It is much easier to use a hand whisk for a small job than to use an electric one which will take time to set up.

Left: Metal fish/egg slices

Right: Tongs for turning meat

Right: Ladles are perfect for serving soup.

Rolling Pins

Although these are usually wooden, those made from marble are ideal for working with pastry as they keep it cool.

Pastry Brushes

Use to brush raw egg on to pastry to give it a golden glow. Pastry brushes are also good for brushing sauces or oil over meat or vegetables, and for greasing or oiling baking trays before you use them.

Pastry Wheel

This is used for making a decoratively cut edge on pastry or stuffed pastas.

Piping/Pastry Bags and Nozzles

A nozzle is dropped into the piping bag until it peeps out of the end. Bigger nozzles are best for piping thicker mixtures such as biscuit (cookie) dough and the smaller ones are best for doing delicate cake or biscuit decorating.

Above: Wooden and marble rolling pins

Luscious Lemon Madeira Cake

This fabulous sugar-crusted cake is soaked in a delicious lemon syrup, so it stays moist and is full of tangy citrus flavour.

You will need

250g/9oz/1 cup plus 2 tbsp
   butter, softened
225g/8oz/generous 1 cup caster
   (superfine) sugar
5 eggs
275g/10oz/2½ cups plain
   (all-purpose) flour, sifted
30ml/2 tbsp baking powder
salt

For the sugar crust

60ml/4 tbsp lemon juice
15ml/1 tbsp golden (light
   corn) syrup
30ml/2 tbsp granulated sugar

Serves 10 🍮🍮🍮

1 Preheat the oven to 180°C/350°F/ Gas 4. Grease a 1kg/2¼lb loaf tin (pan). Beat the butter and sugar together until light and creamy, then gradually beat in the eggs.

2 Mix the flour, baking powder and salt in a bowl and fold in. Spoon into the tin, level the top and bake for 1¼ hours, until a skewer pushed into the middle comes out clean.

Handy hint
Make two cakes. Leave out the sugar crust from one, then cool, wrap and freeze it to eat later.

3 Remove the cake from the oven and stab a skewer right the way through in several places. Warm the lemon juice and syrup, add the sugar and immediately spoon over the cake, so the syrup soaks through but leaves some sugar crystals on the top. Chill the cake before serving.

Chopping Boards

Many cooks use the same board for all their preparation, but it's more hygienic to use a different one for each type of job. It is possible to buy chopping boards with different coloured handles, so the same one is always used for the same job. Scrub boards well after use and always make sure the board has dried properly before you pack it in the cupboard.

Graters

A pyramid or box-shaped grater is the most useful type of grater. Each side has a different grating surface, made up of small, curved, raised blades. Use the coarsest side for bigger vegetables and cheese and the finer sides for grating orange and lemon rind. Stand the grater on a flat surface while you use it, and the grated food will collect inside the pyramid. Always scrub the grater well with a hard brush after use.

Wire Racks

The best way to cool all baked pastries, pies and biscuits (cookies) is to rest them on a wire rack. As the rack is raised, it allows the air to circulate, preventing the base of the cooked food from becoming soggy.

Below: A pyramid grater is easy to use.

Above: Sets of standard cups and spoons for measuring ingredients

Bowls

Mixing bowls come in all sorts of sizes and can be made from plastic and glass. The most useful bowls are made from heatproof glass as they can also be used on the hob (stovetop). Use large bowls for making bread and pastry or for whisking egg whites. Smaller ones should be used for beating eggs and mixing small quanties of dips.

Above: Chopping boards

Timers

Use a timer to ensure that your food cooks for the correct length of time. Most cookers have built-in timers but if yours doesn't, always use a small egg timer for short cooking times as large timers are not very accurate for shorter times.

Measuring Equipment

Most homes have some sort of measuring equipment, whether this is scales, spoons or cups. Recipes have different weights listed because many countries use different ways to measure things. Always stick to the same type of measurements for each recipe. In this book, the metric quantity is given first, such as 115g, followed by the imperial measurement, for example: 4oz. These are used to measure dry ingredients. When you measure liquids, such as oil or milk, there are three different measurements to choose from. The metric measurement, such as 300ml, followed by the imperial, for example: ½ pint, and finally the American measure – 1¼ cups. Most modern measuring jugs have all the measurements written on the side for easy measuring. Small amounts of both dry and wet ingredients are often measured in millilitres (ml) and tablespoons (tbsp). Remember that 15ml is the same as 1 tablespoon and 5ml is the same as 1 teaspoon (tsp). Spoons should be level unless the recipe calls for a heaped spoon.

Banana Gingerbread

This improves with keeping. You can store it in a covered container for up to two months — if you can bear to leave it that long.

You will need

200g/7oz/1¾ cups plain (all-purpose) flour
10ml/2 tsp bicarbonate of soda (baking soda)
10ml/2 tsp ground ginger
175g/6oz/1¼ cups rolled oats
50g/2oz/¼ cup dark brown sugar
75g/3oz/6 tbsp margarine
150g/5oz/⅔ cup golden (light corn) syrup
1 egg, beaten
3 ripe bananas, mashed
75g/3oz/¾ cup icing (confectioners') sugar
preserved stem ginger, to decorate

Makes 12 squares 🍪🍪🍪

1 Preheat the oven to 160°C/325°F/ Gas 3. Lightly grease and line an 18 × 28cm/7 × 11in cake tin (pan).

2 Sift together the flour, bicarbonate of soda and ground ginger, then stir in the rolled oats. Melt the sugar, margarine and syrup in a pan, then stir into the flour mixture. Beat in the egg and mashed bananas.

Handy hint
This cake is ideal for school lunches, as it doesn't break up.

3 Spoon into the prepared tin, level the surface and bake for about 1 hour, or until it feels firm to the touch. leave to cool in the tin, then turn out and cut into squares.

4 Sift the icing sugar into a bowl and stir in just enough water to make a smooth, runny glaze. Drizzle the glaze over each square and top with pieces of chopped ginger, if you like.

Baking Sheets

Use baking sheets as a base for meringues and biscuits (cookies). If you need to use two trays, before you preheat the oven, make sure that they can both fit in the oven at the same time.

Muffin Trays

These look like baking sheets but they have dents in which to spoon the muffin mixture or to fit paper cases for fairy cakes.

Gratin Dishes

These are shallow, ovenproof dishes and are perfect for most baked dishes, such as toad-in-the-hole, shepherd's pie or desserts such as apple pie.

Ramekins

These miniature soufflé dishes are perfect for making individual mousses or baked custards. You can either serve the food in the ramekin or use it as a mould, carefully turning out the food for serving.

Casseroles

These are ovenproof dishes with lids. Flameproof casseroles can also be used on the hob (stovetop).

Pans

Most kitchens have a selection of several different size pans, and may also have some special pans for steaming or melting chocolate. Choosing the right pan for the job is important. If it is too small, then the contents might overflow or they could be packed so tightly that they do not cook properly. If it is too big, the liquid will evaporate too quickly and the dish will dry out.

If you have to stir the mixture while it is cooking, choose a pan with plenty of room for the spoon and for moving the ingredients about without splashing them all over the cooker.

Saucepans

These can be made from many different metals but the most popular saucepans are made from aluminium or stainless steel. They are perfect for sauces, and can also be used for cooking small quantities of food.

Below: Gratin dishes are best for dishes that need to be baked.

Frying Pans

These are the most useful pans found in the kitchen. Some come with a non-stick coating, which is not only healthier because you need less fat, but also easier to clean.

Griddles

These cast-iron cooking pans are flat with deep ridges and are used for cooking on the hob (stovetop). Griddling your food gives it a delicious smoky flavour and it is healthier than frying because the fat will drip off the food and stay between the ridges of the pan.

Woks

These large, deep pans are excellent for making stir-fries. Those with two handles can also be used to deep-fry or steam food.

Steamers

These can be made from stainless steel or bamboo. The Chinese bamboo steamers are especially useful because you can stack one on top of the other so that several layers of food can be cooked at the same time.

Above: Stainless steal steamers are excellent for cooking vegetables.

Carrot Cake

A healthy and tasty cake packed with fruit (figs and bananas) and vegetables (carrots) – topped with a creamy cheese icing to finish it off.

You will need

225g/8oz/2 cups self-raising
   (self-rising) flour
10ml/2 tsp baking powder
150g/5oz/⅔ cup soft brown sugar
115g/4oz ready-to-eat dried figs,
   coarsely chopped
225g/8oz carrots, grated
2 small ripe bananas, mashed
2 eggs
150ml/¼ pint/⅔ cup sunflower oil
175g/6oz/¾ cup cream cheese
175g/6oz/1½ cups icing
   (confectioners') sugar, sifted
small coloured sweets (candies), nuts
   or grated chocolate, to decorate

Serves 10–12 🍴🍴🍴

1 Lightly grease an 18cm/7in round, loose-based springform cake tin (pan). Cut a piece of baking parchment to fit the base of the tin. Preheat the oven to 180°C/350°F/ Gas 4. Put the flour, baking powder and sugar into a large bowl and mix well. Stir in the figs.

2 Using your hands, squeeze as much liquid out of the grated carrots as you can and add them to the bowl. Mix in the mashed bananas. Beat the eggs and oil together and pour them into the mixture. Beat together with a wooden spoon.

3 Spoon into the prepared tin and level the top with a palette knife or metal spatula. Cook for 1–1¼ hours, until a skewer pushed into the centre of the cake comes out clean. Remove the cake from the tin and leave to cool on a wire rack.

4 Beat the cream cheese and icing sugar together, to make a smooth and thick icing. Spread it evenly over the top of the cake. Decorate the top with small coloured sweets, nuts or grated chocolate. Cut in small wedges, to serve.

Getting Switched On

Many of the jobs in the kitchen that take a lot of time can be done using powered tools. As these appliances can be dangerous, always ask an adult to help you.

Blenders

Also called liquidizers, these are sometimes attached to a food processor. They are ideal for turning things into liquid such as fruit for sauces, soups and milk shakes. Hand-held blenders are much smaller and can be used in a small bowl or mug.

Food Processors

This is a giant blender, with a large bowl and many different attachments. The metal chopping blade is used most often and it's best for dry ingredients, such as vegetables. The plastic blade should be used for batters and cakes. Some processors also have grating blades and slicing plates.

Below: A blender (left) and a food processor

Right: A free-standing electric mixer with attachments

Electric Mixers and Whisks

These are like balloon whisks and they can either be free-standing or hand-held. They are used to beat air into mixtures and are better for thicker mixures or larger quantities. They can also blend things together and make them smooth, such as sauces and pastes.

Electric Juicers

These machines extract the juice from fruit and vegetables. To use most modern juicers, you just need to cut the fruit or vegetables and the juicer will separate out the skin and fibre.

Sandwich Makers

These make excellent toasted sandwiches and can be used with many types of bread, packed with your favourite filling. Once it is cooked, leave the sandwich to cool, so that you don't burn your mouth on it.

Mincers/Grinders

There are several types of mincers available. The more old-fashioned ones need to be turned by hand and the more modern mincers are electric. Never use a mincer without an adult's help and keep your fingers well clear of them, even when switched off.

Deep-fat Fryers

These heat oil so that you can fry food safely at the right temperature. Hot oil is dangerous, so always ask an adult to help you to use the fryer.

Simple Chocolate Cake

An easy, everyday chocolate cake that can be filled with buttercream, or with whipped cream for a special occasion.

You will need

115g/4oz plain (semisweet)
chocolate, broken into squares
45ml/3 tbsp milk
75g/3oz/⅔ cup unsalted (sweet)
butter or margarine, softened
200g/7oz/scant 1 cup light
brown sugar
3 eggs
200g/7oz/1¾ cups self-raising
(self-rising) flour
15ml/1 tbsp (unsweetened)
cocoa powder

For the buttercream

75g/3oz/6 tbsp unsalted (sweet)
butter or margarine, softened
175g/6oz/1½ cups icing
(confectioners') sugar
15ml/1 tbsp (unsweetened)
cocoa powder
2.5ml/½ tsp vanilla essence (extract)
icing (confectioners') sugar and
(unsweetened) cocoa powder, for
dusting

Serves 6–8 🍴🍴🍴

1 Preheat the oven to 180°C/350°F/ Gas 4. Grease two 18cm/7in round cake tins (pans) and line the base of each with greaseproof (waxed) paper. Melt the chocolate with the milk in a heatproof bowl set on top of a pan of simmering water. Remove the bowl from the heat.

2 Put the butter and sugar in a mixing bowl and beat together until pale and fluffy. Add the eggs, one at a time, beating well after each addition. Stir in the chocolate mixture until it is well combined.

3 Sift the flour and cocoa over the mixture and fold in with a metal spoon until evenly mixed. Scrape into the prepared pans, smooth to level the surface and bake for 35–40 minutes, or until well risen and firm. Turn out on wire racks and leave to cool.

4 To make the buttercream, beat the butter, icing sugar, cocoa powder and vanilla together in a bowl until the mixture is smooth. Sandwich the cake layers together with the buttercream. Dust the top with a mixture of sieved icing sugar and cocoa before serving.

Cookers

There are many different types of cookers and they run on different types of energy. This is the reason why most recipes have a choice of three settings for using the oven, for example, 200°C/400°F/Gas 6. If you have an electric cooker that works at centigrade temperature (°C), use the first number listed in the heating instructions. For an electric cooker that uses degrees fahrenheit (°F), use the second number and for a gas cooker use the last number.

Most ovens are hottest on the top shelf, but most things are best cooked on the middle one. If two baking trays are being used at the same time, the one nearer the top of the oven will usually be cooked more quickly.

When the recipe says to preheat the oven, it should take about 10 minutes to reach the specified temperature; if you put the food in before the oven is hot enough, it will take longer to cook and the food may not cook properly.

Cookers usually have three different cooking places – the oven, the grill (broiler) and the hob (stovetop).

In the Oven

The oven cooks large items of food slowly and evenly, with the minimum of attention.

Under the Grill/Broiler

The grill cooks quickly, so grilled food must be fairly small and thin or the outside will burn before the middle is properly cooked. You must keep a watch on the food as it will need to be turned often to stop it from burning.

On the Hob/Stovetop

The hob is the burners or hot plates on the top of the oven. The hob can also be separate from the oven.

The control-knobs can be turned up to cook food more quickly, or turned down low to cook food more slowly. You should use saucepans or frying pans to cook food on the hob.

Energy Conservation Tips

Follow these simple rules to save energy and cut fuel bills:
◆ Only use as much water as you need in pans and kettles.
◆ Put lids on pans to bring water and other liquids to the boil. Reduce the heat once the contents have come to the boil.
◆ Flames that lick up the sides of a pan are not only wasting energy, but are also extremely dangerous, so adjust the flame.
◆ Try to cook more than one thing in the oven at a time.

Above: Always use protective oven gloves when taking things out of the oven or microwave.

Microwave Ovens

This small oven is useful for some types of cooking, especially as it cooks quickly. Although powered by electricity, it cooks in a different way to ordinary ovens. Food is cooked from the outside first, so it often needs stirring part of the way through to spread the heat evenly. Most microwaves cannot turn food brown, however, so you'll need to use the grill (broiler) for this. Microwaves are also perfect for thawing out frozen food, reheating cooked food and baking potatoes. Some foods, such as pastry, do not reheat well in microwave ovens as they tend to go soggy. It is always best to reheat pizzas, tarts and quiches in an ordinary oven.

Chocolate Dominoes

Great fun to make and decorate, these novelty sponge cake bars are ideal for birthday parties, though a bit too sticky to play dominoes with.

2 Put margarine, sugar, flour, cocoa powder and eggs in a bowl and beat well until thoroughly mixed and smooth. Spoon into the prepared cake tin and level the surface with a palette knife or metal spatula. Bake for about 30 minutes, until the cake springs back when pressed with the fingertips.

3 Cool in the tin for 5 minutes, then loosen the edges with a knife and transfer to a wire rack. Peel off and throw away the paper and leave the cake to cool completely. Turn the cake on to a chopping board and cut into 16 even-size bars.

You will need

175g/6oz/¾ cup soft margarine

175g/6oz/¾ cup caster (superfine) sugar

150g/5oz/1¼ cups self-raising (self-rising) flour

25g/1oz/¼ cup (unsweetened) cocoa powder, sifted

3 eggs

For the topping

175g/6oz/¾ cup butter

25g/1oz/¼ cup (unsweetened) cocoa powder

300g/11oz/2½ cups icing (confectioners') sugar

a few liquorice strips and 115g/4oz candy-coated chocolate drops

Makes 16 👕👕👕

1 Preheat the oven to 180°C/350°F/ Gas 4. Brush an 18 × 28cm/ 7 × 11in baking tin (pan) with a little vegetable oil and line the base of the tin with greaseproof (waxed) paper.

Try this

To make Traffic Light Cakes, omit the (unsweetened) cocoa and add an extra 25g/1oz/¼ cup plain (all-purpose) flour. Omit cocoa from the topping and add an extra 25g/1oz/¼ cup sugar and 2.5ml/½ tsp vanilla essence (extract). Spread over the cakes and decorate with halved red, yellow and green glacé (candied) cherries to look like traffic lights.

4 To make the topping, place the butter in a bowl, sift in the cocoa and icing sugar and beat until smooth. Spread the topping evenly over the cakes with a spatula. Add a strip of liquorice to each cake and decorate with candy-coated chocolate drops for domino dots.

Techniques

Preparing ingredients is easy when you follow these step-by-step instructions. Be very careful with knives and always rest the ingredients on a chopping board.

Preparing Onions

Using onions of a similar size means they all take the same time to cook.

1 Cut the onion in half with the skin still on. Lay the cut side flat on a board. Trim off both ends. then peel off the skin.

2 To slice the onions, place the peeled halves, cut-side down, on the board. Then hold down each half firmly and cut down to make slices. Do the same with the other half.

4 Then, make cuts at right angles to the first ones, at the same distance apart. The onion will be finely chopped.

3 To chop the onions, make several parallel cuts lengthways (from trimmed end to end), but not cutting right through to one end.

Handy hint
To stop yourself from crying when working with onions, chill the onions before you use them.

Preparing Carrots

Although they are often just sliced into rounds, carrots can look much more attractive if they are cut in a different way.

1 Peel the carrot using a swivel peeler and trim off the ends.

2 Cut the carrot into short lengths and then into thin slices, lengthways. You will need a sharp knife for this job, so keep your fingers well away from the blade of the knife.

3 For slices, cut each thin slice of carrot into fine strips, about the size of matches.

Chocolate Butterscotch Bars

Nutty chocolate shortbread is topped with a thick, creamy layer of butterscotch and a layer of plain chocolate – pure magic.

You will need

225g/8oz/2 cups plain
  (all-purpose) flour
2.5ml/½ tsp baking powder
115g/4oz/½ cup unsalted (sweet)
  butter, chopped
50g/2oz/⅓ cup light muscovado
  (brown) sugar
150g/5oz plain (semisweet)
  chocolate, melted
30ml/2 tbsp ground almonds

For the topping

175g/6oz/¾ cup unsalted
  (sweet) butter
115g/4oz/½ cup caster
  (superfine) sugar
30ml/2 tbsp golden (light
  corn) syrup
175ml/6fl oz/¾ cup condensed milk
150g/5oz/1¼ cups whole
  toasted hazelnuts
225g/8oz plain (semisweet)
  chocolate, chopped

Makes 24 🍪🍪

1 Preheat the oven to 160°C/325°F/ Gas 3. Lightly grease a shallow 30 × 20cm/12 × 8in cake tin (pan).

2 Sift the flour and baking powder into a large bowl. Add the butter and rub it in with your fingertips until the mixture resembles coarse breadcrumbs, then stir in the sugar. Finally, work in the chocolate and ground almonds.

3 Press the mixture evenly into the prepared cake tin and prick the surface with a fork and bake for 25–30 minutes, until firm. Remove from the oven and leave to cool in the tin.

4 To make the topping, mix the butter, sugar, golden syrup and condensed milk in a pan. Heat gently until the butter and sugar have melted. Simmer, stirring occasionally, until golden, then stir in the hazelnuts. Pour the mixture over the cooked base and spread out evenly. Leave to set.

5 Melt the chocolate in a heatproof bowl set on top of a pan of hot water. Spread the melted chocolate over the butterscotch layer. Leave to set before cutting into bars.

Using a Grater

The most popular grater is the pyramid or box type, which offers different-sized blades for grating. Beware of grating your fingers. A rotary grater prevents this and is also ideal for grating chocolate.

1 The very fine side is for grating whole nutmeg. Hold the nutmeg in one hand and rub it up and down the grater. Sometimes, it is easier to do this directly over the food.

2 The medium blades are best for grating citrus rind. The blades only work downwards. You might need to brush some of the grated rind from the inside with a dry pastry brush.

Grating Fresh Root Ginger

Ground ginger is fine in cakes and desserts, but when it comes to a stir-fry, fresh ginger must be used.

1 The quantity is often given as a measurement in centimetres or inches, because the root is long and difficult to weigh accurately. Break off about the quantity you need.

2 Use a peeler, or sharp knife if the ginger is really lumpy, and cut away the tough outer layer.

3 The coarsest side is best for cheese, fruit and vegetables. The blades work when you press downwards and the food will collect inside the grater.

3 Grate on the coarsest side of the grater and use the strips for your recipe. Don't use any stringy pieces.

Chunky Choc Bars

A no-cook, chocolate fruit and nut cake that's a smash-hit with everyone. It's very quick and easy to make, but you must give it time to set.

You will need

350g/12oz plain
    (semisweet) chocolate
115g/4oz/½ cup butter
400g/14oz can condensed milk
225g/8oz digestive biscuits (Graham
    crackers), broken
50g/2oz/⅓ cup raisins
115g/4oz ready-to-eat dried
    peaches, coarsely chopped
50g/2oz/½ cup hazelnuts or pecans,
    coarsely chopped

Makes 12 👤👤

1 Line an 18 × 28cm/7 × 11in cake tin (pan) with clear film (plastic wrap). Melt the chocolate and butter in a bowl over a pan of hot water.

2 Beat the condensed milk into the chocolate and butter mixture. Add the biscuits, raisins, peaches and nuts and mix well, until all the ingredients are coated in chocolate.

3 Tip the mixture into the prepared tin, making sure it is pressed well into the corners. Leave the top craggy. Put in the refrigerator and leave to set.

4 Lift the cake out of the tin using the clear film and then peel it off. Cut into 12 bars and keep chilled until you are ready to eat it.

Grating Lemon Rind and Squeezing Lemon Juice

Recipes sometimes call for the grated rind and juice of lemons or oranges.

1 Rinse the lemon, unless it is labelled unwaxed. Rub the lemon up and down the fine grating side of the grater, until the yellow rind has come off. Keep moving the lemon round, until all the yellow rind is off. Stop grating once the white pith underneath shows through.

2 Cut the lemon in half crossways. Press one half down on to the pointed part of the squeezer and twist. Keep pressing and twisting and the juice will come out of the lemon. The larger pips (seeds) all collect at the base and are held back by the glass (sometimes plastic) "teeth".

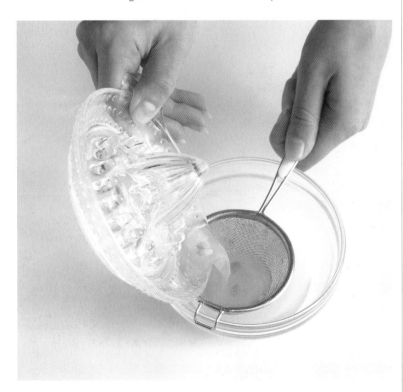

3 Smaller pips might sneak through. Either fish them out with a spoon or your fingers, or pour the juice through a small sieve or strainer, before using it.

Separating Eggs

Meringues and some sauces call for egg whites only, so they must be separated from the yolk.

1 Carefully crack the shell and break the egg on to a saucer.

2 Stand an egg cup over the yolk and hold it firmly in place, taking care not to break the yolk.

3 Hold the saucer over a mixing bowl and let the egg white slide in, holding on to the egg cup. The yolk will be left on the saucer. Don't throw the yolk away– it may be needed later, or you can use it for another recipe.

Pecan Squares

Halved pecan nuts are mixed with sugar and honey and baked in a pastry crust in this sweet treat. Serve with cream as a dessert or on its own for an after-school snack.

You will need
225g/8oz/2 cups plain
    (all-purpose) flour
pinch of salt
115g/4oz/½ cup granulated sugar
225g/8oz/1 cup cold butter or
    margarine, chopped into
    small pieces
1 egg
finely grated rind of 1 lemon

For the topping
175g/6oz/¾ cup butter
75g/3oz/⅓ cup clear honey
50g/2oz/¼ cup granulated sugar
115g/4oz/½ cup dark
    brown sugar
75ml/5 tbsp whipping cream
450g/1lb/4 cups pecan halves

Makes 36 🍴🍴

1 Preheat the oven to 190°C/375°F/ Gas 5. Lightly grease a 37 × 27 × 2.5cm/14½ × 10½ × 1in Swiss (jelly) roll tin (pan).

2 Sift the flour and salt into a mixing bowl. Stir in the sugar. Add the butter or margarine and rub in with your fingertips or a pastry blender until the mixture resembles coarse breadcrumbs. Add the egg and lemon rind and blend well with a fork until the mixture just holds together.

3 Spoon the mixture into the prepared tin. With floured fingertips, press into an even layer. Prick the pastry all over with a fork and chill for 10 minutes. Bake the pastry crust for 15 minutes. Remove the tin from the oven, but keep the oven on while you make the topping.

4 To make the topping, melt the butter, honey and both kinds of sugar in a heavy pan over a low heat, stirring frequently. Increase the heat to medium and bring to the boil. Boil, without stirring, for 2 minutes. Remove the pan from the heat, stir in the cream and pecans. Pour the mixture over the crust, return to the oven and bake for 25 minutes. Leave to cool.

5 When cool, run a knife around the edge of the tin to loosen the pastry. Invert on to a baking sheet, place another baking sheet on top and invert again. Dip a sharp knife into very hot water and cut into squares for serving.

Whipping Cream

Cream can be bought in various thicknesses, so for whipping choose double (heavy), extra-thick or whipping cream, if your recipe needs it. Don't try whipping single (light) cream, as it won't work.

Lining a Tin

Stop cakes sticking to the tin (pan) by lining it with baking parchment or greaseproof (waxed) paper.

1 Stand the tin on the paper and draw around the base. Cut out the shape, just inside the line.

1 Pour the cream into a bowl with plenty of room and use an electric mixer to whip the cream. Keep the electric mixer moving around the bowl as you whisk to make sure it's whisked evenly.

2 Wrap a strip of paper around the outside of the tin and cut it 5cm/2in longer and 5cm/2in deeper than the tin.

2 A hand-held whisk also works well but it takes much longer and makes your arm tired. The cream will first reach a soft and floppy stage, then get thicker the more you whisk.

3 Once whisk lines are left in the cream and it looks fairly stiff, you can stop whipping. Over-whipped cream will curdle and looks like mashed potato.

3 Fold one long edge over by 2.5cm/1in. Make diagonal cuts up to the fold. Grease the tin lightly. Put the long strip inside the tin, around the edges. Lay the round piece on top.

Sticky Date and Apple Squares

If you can resist temptation, keep these fruity squares for one or two days before cutting – the flavour gets even better with time.

2 Add the dates and cook, stirring frequently, until they have softened. Gradually work in the oats, flour, apples and lemon juice, stirring until well mixed.

3 Spoon the mixture into the prepared tin and spread it out evenly. Top with the walnut halves. Bake for 30 minutes, then reduce the oven temperature to 160°C/325°F/ Gas 3 and bake for 10–12 minutes more, until the top feels firm when you touch it and it has turned golden.

4 Cut into squares or bars while still warm if you are going to eat it straight away. Otherwise, leave to cool in the tin, then turn out, wrap in foil when nearly cold. The squares will keep for about 2 days – if you can wait that long!

You will need

115g/4oz/½ cup margarine

50g/2oz/4 tbsp soft dark brown sugar

50g/2oz/4 tbsp golden (light corn) syrup

115g/4oz/⅔ cup chopped dates

115g/4oz/1⅓ cup rolled oats

115g/4oz/1 cup wholemeal self-raising (whole-wheat self-rising) flour

2 eating apples, peeled, cored and grated

5–10ml/1–2 tsp lemon juice

walnut halves, to decorate

Makes 16 🐵🐵

1 Preheat the oven to 190°C/375°F/ Gas 5. Line an 18–20cm/7–8in square or rectangular loose-based cake tin (pan). In a large pan, gently heat the margarine, sugar and syrup together, stirring frequently with a wooden spoon until the margarine has melted completely.

Handy hint

If you have run out of or can't find wholemeal (whole-wheat) self-raising (self-rising) flour, use plain (all-purpose) wholemeal flour and add 5ml/1 tsp baking powder.

Something on the Side

Many dishes need something to go with them, to turn them into a complete meal. Here are some quick easy ideas for accompaniments.

Making Mashed Potatoes

Check the labelling on the bags to see which potatoes are good for mashing, or ask your greengrocer.

You will need

450g/1lb potatoes, peeled
  and quartered
25g/1oz/2 tbsp butter
30ml/2 tbsp milk or cream
salt and ground black pepper

Serves 4

1 Choose a large pan with enough room to mash the potatoes. Add the potatoes, cover them with cold water, add a little salt and bring the water to the boil. Turn down the heat and simmer for 20–25 minutes. When cooked the potatoes will feel tender when you stick a sharp knife in them.

2 Drain the potatoes in a colander and return them to the pan. Add the butter, milk or cream and black pepper and use a potato masher to squash the potatoes and flatten all the lumps. Add more milk if you like them really soft.

Cooking Rice

Measure rice in a jug or measuring cup, by volume rather than by weight, for best results.

You will need

10ml/2 tsp oil
150ml/¼ pint/⅔ cup long grain rice
300ml/½ pint/1¼ cups boiling water
  or stock
salt

Serves 2

1 Heat the oil in a pan and add the rice. Stir well to coat all the grains with the oil.

2 Pour in the boiling water or stock, add a little salt and stir once, before putting on the lid. Turn down the heat so the liquid is just simmering gently. Leave it alone for 15 minutes.

3 Lift the lid carefully and check whether the rice is tender and that the liquid has almost gone. Stir with a fork to fluff up the grains and serve.

Oat and Apricot Clusters

Here is a variation on an old favourite that you can easily make yourself. Check you've got plenty of dried fruits and nuts ready to add before you start.

You will need

50g/2oz/¼ cup butter or margarine
50g/2oz/¼ cup clear honey
40g/2oz/½ cup medium oatmeal
40g/2oz/½ cup chopped ready-to-eat
   dried apricots
15ml/1 tbsp dried banana chips
15ml/1 tbsp dried shreds of coconut
40–75g/2–3oz/2–3 cups cornflakes
   or puffed rice breakfast cereal

Makes 12 🍴🍴

1 Place the butter or margarine and honey in a small pan and warm over a low heat, stirring until the butter or margarine has melted.

2 Remove the pan from the heat and add the oatmeal, dried apricots, banana chips, coconut and cornflakes or rice cereal and mix well with a wooden spoon.

3 Spoon the mixture into 12 paper cake cases, piling it up roughly. Transfer to a baking sheet or a tray, and chill until set and firm.

Handy hint
Make sure that you use ready-to-eat dried apricots, which are usually sold in foil pouches and can be bought in supermarkets and health-food stores. These are different from ordinary dried apricots – usually sold in transparent packets – which have to be soaked before they can be used for cooking and would be too chewy for this recipe.

Cooking Pasta

Pasta comes in loads of different shapes, sizes and colours. Green pasta has spinach in it, red pasta has tomato and brown pasta is made from wholemeal (whole-wheat) flour. Egg pasta has extra eggs in the dough. If it is the main ingredient allow about 75g/3oz dried pasta per person. Use a little less if it is to accompany a meal, although this may vary depending on how hungry you are.

You will need
350–450g/12oz–1lb dried pasta
salt

Serves 4

1 Bring a large pan of water to the boil. Add a little salt. Add the pasta to the pan, a little at a time, so that the water continues to boil.

2 Cook for the time stated on the packet. This will depend on what type of pasta you are using – spaghetti will not take so long as the thicker penne pasta. Fresh pasta cooks very quickly. It should be *al dente* when cooked, which means it still has some firmness to it and isn't completely soft and soggy.

3 Drain the pasta well in a colander and tip it back in to the pan. Pour a sauce over or toss in a little melted butter or a splash of olive oil.

Making Salad Dressing

Green or mixed salads add crunch and freshness to heavy, meaty meals such as lasagne or barbecued ribs, but they are bland and boring without a dressing like this one.

You will need
15ml/1 tbsp white wine vinegar
10ml/2 tsp coarse-grain mustard
30ml/2 tbsp vegetable oil
salt and ground black pepper

Serves 4

1 Put the white wine vinegar and mustard in a small bowl or jug (pitcher). Whisk well with a balloon whisk, then add a little salt and pepper and whisk briefly again.

2 Add the oil slowly, about 5ml/1 tsp at a time, whisking constantly. Pour the dressing over the salad just before serving so that the leaves stay crisp. Use two spoons to toss the salad and coat it with the dressing.

Chewy Fruit Muesli Slice

An easy recipe that needs just measuring out, mixing and baking. The slices are ideal for taking on a picnic or for a school lunch.

You will need

75g/3oz/½ cup ready-to-eat dried
   apricots, chopped
1 eating apple, cored and grated
150g/5oz/1¼ cups Swiss-style
   muesli (granola)
150ml/¼ pint/⅔ cup apple juice
15g/½oz/1 tbsp soft
   sunflower margarine

Makes 8 🕐🕐

1 Preheat the oven to 190°C/375°F/ Gas 5. Place all the ingredients in a large bowl and mix well.

2 Press the mixture evenly into a 20cm/8in non-stick sandwich tin (layer pan) with a wooden spoon and bake for 35–40 minutes, until lightly browned and firm.

3 Remove the tin from the oven and mark the muesli slice into eight wedges with a sharp knife and leave to cool in the tin. Cut along the marked lines to serve.

Breakfast and Brunch

Fruit and Nut Clusters

This is a great recipe to make with little children as there's very little cooking involved – ask your younger brothers or sisters if they'd like to help you.

You will need
225g/8oz white chocolate
50g/2oz/⅓ cup sunflower seeds
50g/2oz/½ cup almond slivers
50g/2oz/4 tbsp sesame seeds
50g/2oz/⅓ cup seedless raisins
5ml/1 tsp ground cinnamon

Makes 24 🍳🍳

Handy hint
Watch the chocolate carefully as it becomes sticky if overcooked.

1 Break the white chocolate into small pieces. Put the chocolate into a heatproof bowl set on top of a pan of hot water over a low heat. Do not let the water touch the base of the bowl, or the chocolate may become too hot.

2 Alternatively, put the chocolate in a microwave-proof bowl and heat it on Medium in the microwave oven for 3 minutes. Stir the melted chocolate until it is smooth and glossy.

3 Mix the sunflower seeds, almond slivers, sesame seeds, raisins and cinnamon together in another bowl, then pour in the melted chocolate and stir well.

4 Using a teaspoon, spoon the mixture into paper sweet (candy) cases and leave in a cool place, but not the refrigerator, to set. Store the clusters in an airtight container in a cool place, separating the layers with greaseproof (waxed) paper.

Citrus Sparkler

Fresh citrus fruits, mixed together, make a simple but thirst-quenching drink. This drink is great on a hot summer day.

You will need

2 oranges
1 lemon
15g/½oz/1 tbsp caster (superfine)
   sugar, or to taste
75ml/5 tbsp water
slices of orange and lemon,
   to decorate

Serves 1 🍴🍴

1 Wash the oranges and lemon and then thinly pare off the rind from the fruit with a sharp knife, leaving the white pith behind. Remove the pith from the fruit and throw it away.

2 Put the orange and lemon rind in a pan with the sugar and water. Heat over a low heat and stir gently until the sugar has dissolved. Remove the pan from the heat and press the rind against the sides of the pan to release all the oils. Cover the pan and cool. Remove and throw away the rind.

3 Process the oranges and lemon to a pulp in a food processor and sweeten the fruit pulp by adding the cooled citrus syrup over the fruit pulp. Leave aside for 2–3 hours for the flavours to infuse (steep).

4 Sieve the fruit pulp, pressing the solids in the sieve to extract as much of the juice as possible. Pour into a tall glass filled with finely crushed ice and decorate with a slice or two of orange and lemon.

Honey and Nut Clusters

These sweet little nibbles will be very popular. To serve, cut in squares or bars and keep in the refrigerator. They are delightfully sticky.

2 Whisk the egg whites in a clean, grease-free bowl until they are stiff, then stir in the chopped nuts.

3 Put the honey and sugar into a small, heavy pan and bring to the boil. Stir in the nut mixture and cook over a medium heat for 10 minutes.

4 Turn the mixture into the tin and level the top with a metal spatula. Cover with non-stick parchment, put weights (such as food cans) on top and chill for at least 2 days.

5 To make little presents, wrap slices in non-stick baking paper and then in gift-wrap, cotton fabric or foil.

You will need

115g/4oz/1 cup blanched almonds
115g/4oz/1 cup shelled hazelnuts
2 egg whites
115g/4oz/½ cup clear honey
115g/4oz/generous ½ cup caster (superfine) sugar

Makes 48 🍪🍪

1 Preheat the oven to the lowest temperature. Line a 20cm/8in square cake tin (pan) with non-stick baking parchment. Spread the almonds and hazelnuts on separate baking sheets and toast in the oven for about 30 minutes. Tip on to a clean dishtowel and rub off the hazelnut skins. Coarsely chop all the nuts.

Handy hint

Honey is always a tricky ingredient to handle and you can end up with a sticky mess all over the kitchen. However, if you dip a spoon in hot water before you scoop the honey out of the jar, it will slide off more easily for measuring. Even better, buy honey in a plastic container that has a pouring hole in the lid. Then you can squeeze out just the quantity you want, where you want it.

Banana Flip

This is a delicious variation on a banana milkshake – it's made with yogurt and sweetened with maple syrup, which has a sweet, nutty flavour.

You will need

1 small banana, peeled and halved
50ml/2fl oz/¼ cup thick Greek
  (US strained plain) yogurt
30ml/2 tbsp maple syrup
5ml/1 tsp lemon juice
2 ice cubes
slice of orange, to serve (optional)

Serves 1 ⑪

1 Put the banana halves, yogurt, maple syrup, lemon juice and the ice cubes into a food processor or blender.

2 Process continuously for about 2 minutes, until the mixture becomes really pale and frothy.

3 Pour the banana flip into a tall, chilled glass and top with a slice of orange to decorate, if you like, then serve immediately.

Try this
For something different, you could swap the banana for a small, peeled, stoned and chopped mango.

Jewelled Christmas Trees

These brightly coloured cookies look wonderful hung on a Christmas tree or in front of a window to catch the light.

You will need

175g/6oz/1½ cups plain
    (all-purpose) flour
75g/3oz/⅓ cup butter, cut into
    small pieces
40g/1½oz/3 tbsp caster
    (superfine) sugar
1 egg white
30ml/2 tbsp orange juice
225g/8oz coloured fruit
    sweets (candies)
coloured ribbons,
    to decorate

Makes 12 🍪🍪🍪

1 Preheat the oven to 180°C/350°F/ Gas 4. Line two baking sheets with non-stick baking parchment. Sift the flour into a mixing bowl. Rub the butter into the flour until the mixture looks like fine breadcrumbs. Stir in the sugar, egg white and enough orange juice to form a soft dough. Knead on a lightly floured surface until smooth.

2 Roll out the dough to about 5mm/ ¼in thick and stamp out as many shapes as possible using a floured Christmas tree cutter. Transfer the shapes to the baking sheets, spacing them well apart because they will spread during cooking. Gather up the trimmings and lightly knead them together until smooth.

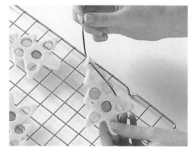

3 Using a 1cm/½in round cutter or the end of a large plain piping nozzle, stamp out and remove six rounds from each tree shape. Cut each sweet into three pieces and place a piece in each hole. Make a small hole at the top of each tree to thread the ribbon through after the cookies have been cooked.

4 Bake for 15–20 minutes, until the biscuits are slightly gold in colour and the sweets have melted and filled the holes. Cool on the baking sheets. Make more biscuits in the same way until you have used up the remaining dough and sweets. Thread short lengths of ribbon through the holes so that the biscuits can be hung up.

Handy hint

You can make other shapes that are also suitable for Christmas decorations or just for a party. Stars and crescent shapes look particularly pretty, but even plain rounds would work well too.

Raspberry and Orange Smoothie

This yummy blend combines the sharp-sweet taste of raspberries and oranges with creamy yogurt. It takes just minutes to prepare – perfect when you're in a hurry.

You will need

250g/9oz/1⅓ cups
    raspberries, chilled
200ml/7fl oz/scant 1 cup natural
    (plain) yogurt, chilled
300ml/½ pint/1¼ cups freshly
    squeezed orange juice, chilled

Serves 2–3 ⓥ

1 Place the raspberries and yogurt in a food processor or blender and process for about 1 minute, until smooth and creamy.

2 Add the orange juice to the mixture and process for about 30 seconds, or until thoroughly mixed. Pour into glasses and serve immediately.

Handy hint
For a super-chilled version of this smoothie, use frozen raspberries instead of fresh. You may need to process the raspberries and yogurt for a little longer to get a really smooth result.

Christmas Cookies

Easy to make, great to give away as presents and delicious to eat yourself – making and decorating these cookies is loads of fun.

You will need

175g/6oz/¾ cup unsalted (sweet) butter
300g/11oz/1½ cups caster (superfine) sugar
1 egg
1 egg yolk
5ml/1 tsp vanilla essence (extract)
grated rind of 1 lemon
pinch of salt
300g/11oz/2½ cups plain (all-purpose) flour

For the decoration (optional)

coloured icing and small sweets (candies) such as silver balls, coloured sugar crystals

Makes 30 🍪🍪

1 Beat the butter until soft with an electric mixer. Gradually add the sugar and continue beating until light and fluffy.

2 Using a wooden spoon, gradually mix in the whole egg and the egg yolk. Add the vanilla essence, lemon rind and salt. Stir to mix well.

3 Sift the flour over the mixture and stir to blend. Gather the dough into a ball, wrap, and chill for 30 minutes.

4 Preheat the oven to 190°C/375°F/Gas 5. Remove the dough from the refrigerator and unwrap, then roll out on a lightly floured surface until about 3mm/⅛in thick.

5 Stamp out shapes, such as Christmas trees, crescents and stars with floured biscuit (cookie) cutters. Alternatively, stamp out plain round cookies.

6 Bake for about 8 minutes, until lightly coloured. Using a palette knife or metal spatula, transfer the cookies to a wire rack and leave to cool completely before decorating, if you like, with icing and sweets.

Apricot and Almond Muesli

This tasty wholegrain fruit and nut muesli, which is packed with fibre, vitamins and minerals, is a great way to start the day.

You will need

115g/4oz/½ cup ready-to-eat
  dried apricots
50g/2oz/½ cup whole
  blanched almonds
200g/7oz/2 cups rolled oats
75g/3oz/scant 1 cup wheatflakes or
  oatbran flakes
50g/2oz/scant ½ cup raisins or
  sultanas (golden raisins)
40g/1½oz/⅓ cup sunflower seeds
milk, natural (plain) yogurt or fresh
  fruit juice, and fresh fruit, to serve

Serves 8 ⓥ

1 Using a sharp knife, cut the ready-to-eat dried apricots into small pieces, all about the same size. Carefully cut the blanched almonds into thin slivers

2 Stir all the ingredients together in a large bowl. Store in an airtight container and eat within 6 weeks.

3 Serve the muesli with milk, natural yogurt or fruit juice and top with fresh fruit, such as slices of peach, banana or strawberries.

Try this
You could add other dried fruits, such as dates, figs, peaches, pears, pineapples or apples.

Marshmallow Crispy Cakes

So easy to make – and even easier to eat – these sticky squares are sure to disappear almost as soon as they have set.

You will need

250g/9oz toffees (taffies)
50g/2oz/4 tbsp butter
45ml/3 tbsp milk
115g/4oz/1 cup marshmallows
175g/6oz/6 cups puffed rice
   breakfast cereal

Makes 45 🎔🎔

1 Lightly brush a 20 × 33cm/ 8 × 13in roasting pan with a little vegetable oil. Put the toffees, butter and milk in a pan and heat gently, stirring until the toffees have melted.

2 Add the marshmallows and cereal and stir until well mixed and the marshmallows have melted.

Handy hint
Melt the mixture over a low heat and stir so it doesn't burn.

3 Spoon the mixture into the prepared roasting pan, level the surface and leave to set.

4 When cool and hard, cut the crispy cakes into squares, carefully remove from the pan, and put into paper cases to serve.

Try this
Experiment by substituting a different type of breakfast cereal for the puffed rice. Try corn flakes, bran flakes or even a cereal mixed with fruit.

Honey-nut Granola

Honey-coated nuts, seeds and oats, combined with sweet dried fruits, make a really great nutritious breakfast. Serve the granola with milk or yogurt and fresh fruit.

You will need

100g/3½oz/1 cup rolled oats
115g/4oz/1 cup jumbo oats
65g/2½oz/½ cup sunflower seeds
30ml/2 tbsp sesame seeds
75g/3oz/½ cup hazelnuts, roasted
25g/1oz/¼ cup almonds,
   coarsely chopped
50ml/2fl oz/¼ cup sunflower oil
50g/2oz/¼ cup clear honey
65g/2½oz/½ cup raisins
65g/2½oz/½ cup dried
   sweetened cranberries

Serves 4 ⦿⦿

1 Preheat the oven to 140°C/ 275°F/Gas 1. Mix together both types of oats, the sunflower and sesame seeds and the hazelnuts and almonds in a large bowl.

2 Gently heat the sunflower oil and honey in a large pan, stirring occasionally, until the honey has melted, then remove the pan from the heat. Add the oats mixture and stir well to mix. Spread out the mixture on one or two baking sheets.

3 Bake for about 50 minutes, until crisp, stirring occasionally to prevent the mixture from sticking to the baking sheet. Remove from the oven and mix in the raisins and cranberries. Leave to cool, then store in an airtight container.

Chocolate Crackle-tops

These scrumptious cookies have a cracked appearance when baked – serve them with vanilla or toffee ice cream for a quick dessert.

You will need

200g/7oz plain (semisweet)
  chocolate, chopped
90g/3½oz/scant ½ cup unsalted
  (sweet) butter
115g/4oz/½ cup caster
  (superfine) sugar
3 eggs
5ml/1 tsp vanilla essence (extract)
215g/7½oz/scant 2 cups plain (all-
  purpose) flour
25g/1oz/¼ cup (unsweetened)
  cocoa powder
2.5ml/½ tsp baking powder
pinch of salt
175g/6oz/1½ cups icing
  (confectioners') sugar, for coating

Makes 38 🍪🍪🍪

1 Melt the chocolate and butter together in a medium pan over a low heat, stirring frequently until smooth. Remove the pan from the heat. Stir in the sugar and keep stirring for 2–3 minutes, until the sugar dissolves. Add the eggs, one at a time, beating well after each addition. Stir in the vanilla.

2 Sift together the flour, cocoa powder, baking powder and salt into a bowl. Gradually stir into the chocolate mixture, in batches, until just blended. Cover the dough with clear film (plastic wrap) and chill for at least 1 hour, until the dough is cold and holds its shape.

3 Preheat the oven to 160°C/ 325°F/Gas 3. Grease two or more large baking sheets. Place the icing sugar in a small, deep bowl. Using a small ice-cream scoop or round teaspoon, scoop cold dough into small balls and roll between the palms of your hands into 4cm/1½in balls.

4 Gently drop each ball into the icing sugar and roll until heavily coated all over. Remove with a slotted spoon and tap gently against the side of the bowl to shake off any excess sugar. Place on the prepared baking sheets about 4cm/1½in apart.

5 Bake for 10–15 minutes, until the tops of the cookies feel just firm when touched with your fingertips. Remove the baking sheets to wire racks and leave them to stand for 2–3 minutes. Then, using a metal palette knife or spatula, carefully remove the cookies to a wire rack to cool completely.

Fruity Sesame Porridge

Oats are incredibly good for you. They provide plenty of energy that is released slowly throughout the morning, so this porridge will help keep you going until lunchtime.

You will need

50g/2oz/scant ½ cup rolled oats

475ml/16fl oz/2 cups milk

75g/3oz/½ cup ready-to-eat dried
   fruit salad, chopped

30ml/2 tbsp sesame seeds, toasted

Serves 2 🍴

1 Put the rolled oats, milk and chopped dried fruit in a non-stick pan. Bring the mixture to the boil, then lower the heat and simmer gently for 3 minutes, stirring occasionally, until thickened. Serve in individual bowls, sprinkled with toasted sesame seeds.

Try this

If you use "old-fashioned" or "original" oats, the porridge will be quite thick and coarse textured. You could also use jumbo oats. However, if you prefer a smoother porridge, use ordinary rolled oats (sometimes called oatflakes).

Double Chocolate Cookies

It's amazing how something that's so simple to make can taste so good. Keep these luscious treats under lock and key unless you're feeling generous.

You will need

115g/4oz/½ cup unsalted
  (sweet) butter
115g/4oz/⅔ cup light muscovado
  (brown) sugar
1 egg
5ml/1 tsp vanilla essence (extract)
150g/5oz/1¼ cups self-raising
  (self-rising) flour
75g/3oz/¾ cup rolled oats
115g/4oz plain (semisweet)
  chocolate, coarsely chopped
115g/4oz white chocolate,
  coarsely chopped

Makes 18–20 🍴🍴

1 Preheat the oven to 190°C/375°F/ Gas 5. Lightly grease two baking sheets. Using a wooden spoon, beat the butter with the sugar in a bowl until the mixture is pale and fluffy. Add the egg and vanilla essence and beat well again.

2 Sift the flour over the mixture and fold in lightly with a metal spoon, then add the oats and chopped plain and white chocolate and stir until evenly mixed.

3 Place small spoonfuls of the mixture in 18–20 rocky heaps on the prepared baking sheets, leaving space for them to spread.

4 Bake for 15–20 minutes, until they begin to turn pale golden. Cool for 2–3 minutes on the baking sheets, then transfer the cookies to wire racks to cool completely.

Handy hint

If you're short of time, substitute chocolate chips for the chopped chocolate. Chopped preserved stem ginger would make a delicious addition as well.

Crunchy Oat, Fruit and Yogurt Layer

Chunks of peach or nectarine and crunchy cereal contrast in texture in this easy and tasty combination. It can be served as a breakfast treat or even as a healthy dessert.

You will need

1 peach or nectarine

75g/3oz/1 cup crunchy toasted oat cereal

150ml/¼ pint/⅔ cup natural (plain) yogurt

15ml/1 tbsp pure fruit jam

15ml/1 tbsp freshly squeezed fruit juice

Serves 2 ⓥ

3 Sprinkle the toasted oat cereal over the fruit in an even layer, then top with the yogurt.

4 Stir the jam and juice together, then drizzle the mixture over the yogurt. Decorate with the saved peach or nectarine and serve immediately.

Handy hint

If you like, use a flavoured toasted oat cereal such as raisin and almond. Any fruit jam and juice, which go with each other and with the fruit, can be used.

1 Halve the peach or nectarine, twist the two halves in opposite directions to separate, and remove the stone (pit) using a teaspoon. Cut the fruit into bitesize pieces with a sharp knife.

2 Share the chopped peach or nectarine between two tall glasses, saving a few pieces for decoration.

Ginger Cookies

This is a really easy biscuit recipe – ideal for beginners. You'll have lots of fun mixing and rolling the dough and cutting out different shapes.

You will need

115g/4oz/²⁄₃ cup soft brown sugar
115g/4oz/½ cup soft margarine
pinch of salt
few drops of vanilla
    essence (extract)
175g/6oz/1¼ cups wholemeal
    (whole-wheat) flour
15g/½oz/1 tbsp (unsweetened)
    cocoa powder, sifted
10ml/2 tsp ground ginger
a little milk
glacé icing (frosting) and glacé
    (candied) cherries, to decorate

Makes 16 🍪🍪

1 Preheat the oven to 190°C/375°F/ Gas 5. Grease a baking sheet. Beat together the sugar, margarine, salt and vanilla until very soft and light.

Handy hint

To make glacé icing (frosting), sift some icing (confectioners') sugar into a bowl and gradually beat in enough hot water to make a smooth icing that will coat the back of a spoon. You will need 30–60ml/2–4 tbsp water for 225g/8oz icing sugar.

2 Work in the flour, cocoa and ginger, adding a little milk, if necessary, to bind the mixture. Knead lightly on a floured surface until smooth.

3 Roll out the dough to about 5mm/ ¼in thick. Stamp out shapes using floured biscuit (cookie) cutters and place on the prepared baking sheet.

4 Bake for 10–15 minutes. Leave to cool on the baking sheets until firm, then transfer to a wire rack to cool completely. Decorate with glacé icing and pieces of glacé cherries.

Breakfast Pizzas

Here is a very simple but tasty breakfast or brunch dish. The combination of cheese, tomato and fresh herbs is popular and is often used on pizza.

You will need

1 ciabatta loaf
4 tomatoes
115g/4oz mozzarella or
  Cheddar cheese
15ml/1 tbsp olive oil
15ml/1 tbsp marjoram
salt and ground black pepper

Serves 2 🍴🍴

Handy hint
Add a sprinkle of fresh chopped marjoram to your favourite pizza topping. Sprinkle over 7.5–15ml/½–1 tbsp. The flavour is strong, so use with care, especially if you haven't tried it before.

1 Preheat the grill (broiler) to high. Cut the ciabatta loaf in half lengthways. Toast it very lightly under the grill until it has turned a pale golden brown.

2 Meanwhile, peel the tomatoes by placing them in boiling water for 30 seconds, then rinsing them under cold running water. The skins should peel off easily. Cut into thick slices.

3 Slice or grate the cheese. Lightly drizzle a little oil over the bread and top with the tomato slices and sliced or grated cheese. Season with salt and ground black pepper and sprinkle the marjoram over the top.

4 Drizzle with a little more olive oil and return to the grill until the cheese bubbles and is just starting to brown. Serve immediately, but take care not to burn your tongue on the cheese.

Peanut Cookies

Packing up a picnic? Got a birthday party coming up? Make sure some of these nutty cookies are on the menu.

You will need

225g/8oz/1 cup butter
30ml/2 tbsp smooth peanut butter
115g/4oz/1 cup icing
    (confectioners') sugar
50g/2oz/scant ½ cup
    cornflour (cornstarch)
225g/8oz/2 cups plain
    (all-purpose) flour
115g/4oz/1 cup unsalted peanuts

Makes 25 👐👐

1 Put the butter and peanut butter in a bowl and beat together. Add the icing sugar, cornflour and plain flour and mix together with your hands to make a soft dough.

2 Preheat the oven to 180°C/ 350°F/Gas 4 and lightly oil two baking sheets. Roll the mixture into 25 small balls, using floured hands, and place them on the baking sheets. Leave room for the cookies to spread.

3 Press the tops of the balls of dough flat using the back of a fork.

Handy hint
Make massive monster cookies by making bigger balls of dough.

4 Press some of the peanuts into each of the cookies. Cook for 15–20 minutes, until lightly browned. Leave to cool for a few minutes before lifting them carefully on to a wire rack with a palette knife or metal spatula. When they are cool, pack them in an airtight container.

Melt-in-the-mouth Tomatoes

Nothing could be simpler than this dish, yet a drizzle of olive oil and balsamic vinegar and shavings of Parmesan cheese transform tomatoes on toast into something special.

You will need

olive oil, for brushing and drizzling
6 tomatoes, thickly sliced
4 thick slices soda bread
balsamic vinegar, for drizzling
salt and ground black pepper
shavings of Parmesan cheese,
     to serve

Serves 4 🍴🍴

1 Brush a ridged griddle pan with a little olive oil and heat. Add the tomato slices and cook over a medium heat for about 4 minutes, turning once, until they are softened and slightly blackened. Alternatively, preheat a grill (broiler) to high and line the rack with foil. Brush the tomato slices with oil and grill (broil) them for 4–6 minutes, turning once and brushing with more oil, until softened.

2 Meanwhile, lightly toast the soda bread until pale golden.

Handy hint

Using a griddle pan is healthier as it reduces the amount of oil required for cooking the tomatoes. It also makes them taste as if they have been cooked on the barbecue – which is fun.

3 Place the tomatoes on top of the toast and drizzle each portion with a little olive oil and balsamic vinegar. Season with salt and ground black pepper to taste and serve immediately with thin shavings of Parmesan.

Try this

• For a more substantial meal, place a couple of slices of prosciutto on the toast before adding the tomatoes.
• This recipe is also delicious with slices of mozzarella cheese instead of the shaved Parmesan.
• Anchovies go well with tomatoes. If you like them, try tearing a few anchovy fillets into thin strips and arranging them on top of the tomatoes. Leave out the Parmesan cheese.

Five Spice Fingers

Light, crumbly biscuits with an unusual Chinese five-spice flavouring, which is a combination of pepper, star anise, cinnamon, fennel seeds and cloves.

2 Add the flour and Chinese five-spice powder and beat again until well mixed and smooth. Spoon the mixture in a large piping (pastry) bag fitted with a large star nozzle.

3 Preheat the oven to 180°C/350°F/Gas 4. Lightly oil two baking sheets and pipe short lines of mixture, about 7.5cm/3in long, on them. Leave enough room for them to spread during cooking. Bake for 15 minutes, until lightly browned. Leave to cool slightly, before lifting them on to a wire rack with a palette knife or metal spatula.

4 Sift the remaining icing sugar into a small bowl and stir in the orange rind. Add enough juice to make a thin icing (frosting) and brush it over the biscuits (cookies) while they are still warm. Leave to cool and set before serving on their own or with ice cream or other creamy desserts.

You will need

115g/4oz/½ cup margarine
50g/2oz/½ cup icing (confectioners') sugar
115g/4oz/1 cup plain (all-purpose) flour
10ml/2 tsp Chinese five-spice powder
vegetable oil, for greasing
grated rind and juice of ½ orange

Makes 28

1 Put the margarine and half the icing sugar in a bowl and beat with a wooden spoon until the mixture is smooth, creamy and soft.

Cheese and Banana Toasties

Toast topped with soft cheese and sliced banana sounds like a funny combination, but it makes the perfect breakfast and is delicious when drizzled with honey.

1 Preheat the grill (broiler). Place the slices of bread on a rack in a grill pan and toast on one side only until golden brown.

2 Turn the bread over and spread the untoasted side of each slice with soft cheese. Sprinkle over the crushed cardamom seeds, if using.

3 Slice the bananas and arrange the slices on top of the cheese, then drizzle each slice with 5ml/1 tsp of the clear honey.

4 Slide the pan back under the medium-hot grill and cook for a few minutes until the topping is bubbling. Serve the hot toasties immediately. Be careful not to burn your mouth on the melted cheese.

You will need

4 thick slices of wholemeal (whole-wheat) bread

115g/4oz/½ cup soft (farmer's) cheese

1.5ml/¼ tsp cardamom seeds, crushed (optional)

4 small bananas, peeled

20ml/4 tsp clear honey

Serves 4 🍴🍴

Try this

For a delicious variation, use fruited, sesame seed or caraway seed bread. Leave out the cardamom seeds and sprinkle cinnamon on the bananas before adding the honey. Single flower honeys are particularly delicious – try orange or lemon blossom.

Gingerbread Teddies

These bears in pyjamas make a perfect gift for friends. If you can't get a large bear cutter, make smaller bears or use a traditional gingerbread-man cutter.

You will need

75g/3oz white chocolate, chopped
175g/6oz ready-to-roll white
   sugar paste
blue food colouring
25g/1oz plain (semisweet) chocolate

For the gingerbread

175g/6oz/1½ cups plain
   (all-purpose) flour
1.5ml/¼ tsp bicarbonate of soda
   (baking soda)
pinch of salt
5ml/1 tsp ground ginger
5ml/1 tsp ground cinnamon
65g/2½oz/⅓ cup unsalted (sweet)
   butter, chopped
75g/3oz/⅓ cup caster (superfine) sugar
30ml/2 tbsp maple or golden (light
   corn) syrup
1 egg yolk, beaten

Makes 6 🐻🐻🐻

1 To make the gingerbread, sift together the flour, bicarbonate of soda, salt and spices into a large bowl. Rub the butter into the flour until the mixture resembles fine breadcrumbs. Stir in the sugar, syrup and egg yolk and mix to a firm dough. Knead lightly. Wrap and chill for 30 minutes.

2 Preheat the oven to 180°C/350°F/ Gas 4. Grease two large baking sheets. Roll out the gingerbread dough on a floured surface and cut out bears, using a floured 13cm/5in biscuit (cookie) cutter.

3 Transfer to the baking sheets and bake for 10–15 minutes, until just beginning to colour around the edges. Leave on the baking sheets for 3 minutes, then transfer to a wire rack.

4 Melt half the white chocolate. Put in a paper piping (pastry) bag and snip off the tip. To make a template for the bears' clothes, draw an outline of the cutter on to paper, finishing at the neck and halfway down the arms and legs.

5 Thinly roll the sugar paste on a surface dusted with icing sugar. Use the template to cut out the clothes, and secure them to the biscuits with melted chocolate.

6 Use the sugar paste trimmings to add ears, eyes and snouts. Dilute the blue colouring with a little water and use it to paint striped pyjamas.

7 Melt the remaining white chocolate and the plain chocolate in separate bowls over pans of hot water. Put in separate paper piping bags and snip off the tips. Pipe a decorative outline around the pyjamas with white chocolate. Use the plain chocolate to pipe the faces.

Caribbean Toasts

Griddling concentrates the sweetness of the pineapple and mango in this recipe, giving the fruits a caramel flavour that goes really well with the vanilla yogurt.

You will need

1 large pineapple
1 large mango
25g/1oz/2 tbsp unsalted (sweet) butter, melted
4 thick slices panettone

For the vanilla yogurt

250g/9oz/generous 1 cup Greek (US strained plain) yogurt
30ml/2 tbsp clear honey
2.5ml/1/2 tsp ground cinnamon
a few drops vanilla essence (extract)

Serves 4 🍴🍴

2 To prepare the mango, use a sharp knife to cut away the two thick sides of the mango as close to the stone (pit) as possible. Peel the mango, then cut as much of the remaining flesh from the stone as possible. Slice the fruit and throw away the stone.

3 Heat a griddle pan over a medium heat. Add the pineapple and mango (you may need to do this in batches). Brush with melted butter and cook for 8 minutes, turning once, until the fruit is soft and slightly golden. Alternatively, heat the grill (broiler) to high and line the rack with foil. Place the pineapple and mango on the foil, brush with butter and grill (broil) for 4 minutes on each side.

4 Meanwhile, place the yogurt in a bowl with the honey, cinnamon and vanilla and stir well. Lightly toast the panettone, top with the griddled pineapple and mango and serve with the bowl of vanilla yogurt.

1 Cut the bottom and the spiky top off the pineapple, then stand it upright and cut off the skin, removing all the spikes, but as little of the flesh as possible. Lay the pineapple on its side and cut into quarters; remove the core if it is hard. Cut the pineapple into thick wedges.

Try this

Place 3 peaches in a bowl of boiling water for 30 seconds. Remove with a slotted spoon and peel. Cut the flesh into slices, away from the stone (pit). Slice 4 plums. Brush the fruit with melted butter and cook as here.

Cookies
and Cakes

Spanish Scramble

This mixture of ripe plum tomatoes, sweet peppers and eggs has all the flavours of the Mediterranean. It is perfect for a weekend brunch.

You will need

60–90ml/4–6 tbsp olive oil
2 small onions, coarsely chopped
4 red or yellow (bell) peppers, seeded and chopped
2 large garlic cloves, finely chopped
pinch of chilli powder (optional)
675g/1½lb ripe plum tomatoes, peeled, seeded and chopped
15ml/1 tbsp chopped fresh oregano or 5ml/1 tsp dried oregano
1 long French stick
25g/1oz/2 tbsp butter
6 eggs, beaten
salt and ground black pepper
fresh basil leaves, to serve

Serves 6 🍴🍴

1 Heat a little oil in a large, heavy frying pan. Add the chopped onions and cook over a gentle heat, stirring occasionally, for about 5 minutes, until softened but not coloured.

2 Add the red or yellow peppers, garlic and chilli powder, if using. Cook for a further 5 minutes, stirring, then add the plum tomatoes, salt, pepper and oregano and cook over a medium heat for 15–20 minutes, until most of the liquid has gone.

3 Preheat the oven to 200°C/400°F/ Gas 6. Cut the bread in half lengthways, trim off the ends, then cut it into six equal pieces and brush with olive oil. Place on baking sheets and bake for 8–10 minutes, until crisp and just turning golden.

4 Heat the butter in a heavy pan until it bubbles. Then add the eggs and stir gently until they have scrambled. Turn off the heat and stir in the tomato mixture. Share the scrambled egg and tomato mixture evenly among the pieces of bread and sprinkle with the basil leaves. Serve immediately or leave to cool slightly and serve warm.

Strawberry Smoothie

So much better than strawberry milkshakes you can buy, this deliciously creamy smoothie is a tangy blend of strawberries, yogurt and milk.

You will need

225g/8oz/2 cups strawberries
150ml/¼ pint/⅔ cup Greek
   (US strained plain) yogurt
475ml/16fl oz/2 cups ice-cold milk
30ml/2 tbsp icing
   (confectioners') sugar

Serves 4–6 ⓘ

1 Save a few of the strawberries for decoration and put the rest in a blender with the yogurt. Process until fairly smooth.

2 Add the milk and icing sugar, process again and pour into glasses. Serve each glass decorated with one or two of the saved strawberries and with drinking straws, if you like.

Bacon, Egg and Mushroom Baps

There's nothing better than a traditional English breakfast. This rather grown-up breakfast bap is best served with your favourite sauce.

You will need

350g/12oz unsmoked bacon
    rashers (strips)
50g/2oz/4 tbsp unsalted (sweet)
    butter, plus extra for spreading
115g/4oz/1½ cups chanterelle
    mushrooms, trimmed and halved
60ml/4 tbsp sunflower oil
4 eggs
4 large baps (rolls), split
salt and ground black pepper

Serves 4 👖👖

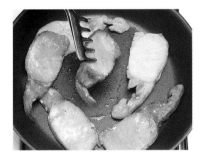

1 Place the bacon in a large, non-stick frying pan and cook in its own fat until crisp. Transfer to a heatproof plate, cover and keep warm in a low oven.

2 Melt 25g/1oz/2 tbsp of the butter in the same frying pan, add the chanterelles and cook over a low heat until soft, without letting them colour. Transfer to a plate, cover and keep warm in the oven with the bacon.

3 Melt the remaining butter in the frying pan, add the oil and heat to a medium temperature. Carefully break the eggs into the pan, two at a time, if necessary. Cook them over a low heat, turning to cook both sides if you like your eggs well done (over easy).

4 Toast the baps, spread with butter, then top each one with bacon, chanterelle mushrooms and a fried egg. Season with salt and ground black pepper, add the bap lids and serve immediately.

Handy hint

These chanterelle mushrooms are very grown-up, but you can use any other kind of mushroom such as brown cap (cremini) mushrooms, chestnut mushrooms or portabello mushrooms.

Cool Crimson Smoothie

The blend of perfectly ripe bananas and creamed coconut gives this drink a fantastic creamy taste that is perfect for after lunch.

You will need

200g/7oz/1¾ cups strawberries, plus extra, sliced, to decorate
2 ripe bananas
115g/4oz/2 cups creamed coconut (coconut cream)
120ml/4fl oz/½ cup water
175ml/6fl oz/¾ cup milk
30ml/2 tbsp lemon juice
10 ice cubes

Serves 4 🍸

1 Rinse the strawberries, if necessary, then remove the leaves and centres. Peel the bananas and cut them into fairly large chunks.

2 Put the strawberries and bananas in a food processor or blender, crumble in the creamed coconut or add the coconut cream and add the water. Process until the mixture is smooth, scraping down the sides of the goblet as necessary.

3 Add the milk, lemon juice and ice cubes, crushing the ice first or use a heavy-duty processor. Process until smooth and thick. Pour into tall glasses and top each with a slice or two of strawberry. Serve the smoothies immediately.

American Pancakes with Bacon

These small, thick, buttery pancakes will be eaten in seconds, so make plenty. The batter can be made the night before, ready for breakfast.

You will need

175g/6oz/1½ cups plain (all-purpose) flour, sifted

pinch of salt

15ml/1 tbsp caster (superfine) sugar

2 large (US extra large) eggs

150ml/¼ pint/⅔ cup milk

5ml/1 tsp bicarbonate of soda (baking soda)

10ml/2 tsp cream of tartar

vegetable oil, for cooking

butter, maple syrup and crisply grilled (broiled) bacon, to serve

Makes about 20 🍴🍴

1 To make the batter, mix the flour, salt and sugar. In a separate bowl, beat the eggs and milk together, then gradually stir into the flour, beating to a smooth, thick consistency. Add the bicarbonate of soda and cream of tartar, mix well, then cover and chill until ready to cook.

2 When you are ready to cook, beat the batter again. Heat a little oil in a heavy frying pan or griddle. Drop dessertspoonfuls of the mixture into the pan, spaced well apart, and cook over a fairly high heat until small bubbles appear on the surface and the undersides are golden brown.

3 Carefully turn the pancakes over with a palette knife or spatula and cook briefly until golden underneath, then transfer them to a heated serving dish. Top each pancake with a little butter and drizzle with maple syrup. Serve with grilled bacon.

Banana-Passion Fruit Shake

This wonderfully frothy shake is surprisingly refreshing. Sparkling mineral water gives a light touch to the creamy blend of banana and yogurt, while passion fruit adds a tang.

You will need

1 ripe banana, peeled
2 passion fruits
150ml/¼ pint/⅔ cup natural
   (plain) yogurt
100ml/3½ fl oz/generous ⅓ cup
   sparkling mineral water
grated nutmeg, to sprinkle (optional)

Serves 2 ⓥ

Try this

To make a mango-passion shake, use a small, very ripe, peeled, stoned (pitted) and chopped mango in place of the banana.

1 Cut the passion fruits in half and, using a tea spoon, scoop the flesh and seeds into a fine sieve.

2 Using the back of the spoon, carefully press the passion fruit flesh through the sieve into a food processor or blender.

3 Cut the banana into fairly large chunks and place in the food processor or blender. Add the yogurt and process for 2 minutes.

4 Pour the shake into two glasses. Add the sparkling water. Sprinkle with nutmeg, if you like, and serve.

Nutty Banana Pancakes

These thick and delicious pancakes are topped with a mouthwatering mixture of maple-syrup-flavoured caramel bananas and pecan nuts.

You will need

75g/3oz/⅔ cup plain
   (all-purpose) flour
50g/2oz/½ cup wholemeal (whole-
   wheat) flour
50g/2oz/scant ½ cup rolled oats
5ml/1 tsp baking powder
pinch of salt
25g/1oz/2 tbsp caster
   (superfine) sugar
1 egg
15ml/1 tbsp sunflower oil, plus extra
   for frying
250ml/8fl oz/1 cup semi-skimmed
   (low-fat) milk

For the caramel bananas and pecan nuts

50g/2oz/¼ cup butter
15ml/1 tbsp maple syrup
3 bananas, halved and
   quartered lengthways
25g/1oz/¼ cup pecan nuts

Serves 4 🍴🍴

2 Heat a large, heavy, lightly oiled frying pan. Using about 30ml/2 tbsp of batter for each pancake, cook two to three pancakes at a time. Cook for 3 minutes on each side, or until golden. Keep warm while you cook the remaining pancakes.

3 To make the caramel bananas and pecan nuts, wipe out the frying pan with a thick wad of kitchen paper, taking care not to burn your hand. Add the butter and heat gently until the butter melts, then stir in the maple syrup. Add the bananas and pecan nuts to the pan.

4 Cook for about 4 minutes, turning once, or until the bananas have just softened and the sauce has turned golden brown and caramelized. To serve, place two pancakes on each of four warm plates and top with the caramel bananas and pecan nuts. Serve immediately.

1 To make the pancakes, mix together both the flours, the oats, baking powder, salt and sugar in a bowl. Make a well in the centre of the flour mixture and add the egg, oil and a quarter of the milk. Mix well, then gradually add the rest of the milk to make a thick batter. Cover and leave to rest for 20 minutes in the refrigerator.

Fruit Crush and Fruit Kebabs

Fruit crush is just the ticket on a sultry summer's day; served with mouthwatering fruit kebabs it makes a delicious and healthy snack – ideal for after school.

You will need

300ml/½ pint/1¼ cups orange juice
300ml/½ pint/1¼ cups
    pineapple juice
300ml/½ pint/1¼ cups tropical
    fruit juice
475ml/16fl oz/2 cups lemonade
    (lemon soda)
fresh pineapple slices and fresh
    cherries, to decorate

For the fruit kebabs

24 small strawberries
24 green seedless grapes
12 marshmallows
1 kiwi fruit, peeled and cut in
    12 wedges
1 banana
15ml/1 tbsp lemon juice

Serves 6 🍸

1 To make the fruit crush, put the orange juice and the pineapple juice into separate ice-cube trays and freeze them until solid.

Handy hint

If you fill the ice cubes trays with the juice in the morning, it will be frozen by the time you get home from school.

2 Mix together the tropical fruit juice and lemonade in a large jug (pitcher). Put a mixture of the ice cubes in each glass and pour the fruit crush over. Decorate the glasses with the pineapple slices and cherries.

3 To make the fruit kebabs, thread two strawberries, two grapes, a marshmallow and a wedge of kiwi fruit on to each of twelve wooden skewers.

4 Peel the banana and cut into twelve slices. Toss it in the lemon juice and thread on to the skewers. Serve immediately.

Try this

If you are making the fruit crush for a party, place tiny wedges of fresh orange and fresh or canned pineapple in the ice cube trays before you pour in the juice.

Cheese and Potato Scones

The unusual addition of creamy mashed potato gives these scones a light, moist crumb and a crisp crust. A sprinkling of Cheddar and sesame seeds adds the finishing touch.

You will need

115g/4oz/1 cup wholemeal (whole-wheat) flour, plus extra for dusting
2.5ml/½ tsp salt
20ml/4 tsp baking powder
40g/1½oz/3 tbsp unsalted (sweet) butter, plus extra for greasing
2 eggs, beaten
50ml/2fl oz/¼ cup semi-skimmed (low-fat) milk or buttermilk
115g/4oz/1½ cups cooked, mashed potato
45ml/3 tbsp chopped fresh sage
50g/2oz/½ cup grated mature (sharp) Cheddar cheese
sesame seeds, for sprinkling

Makes 9 🐟🐟

1 Preheat the oven to 220°C/425°F/ Gas 7. Grease a baking sheet. Sift the flour, salt and baking powder into a bowl. Rub in the butter with your fingers until the mixture looks like breadcrumbs. Mix in half the eggs and all the milk or buttermilk. Add the potato, sage and half the Cheddar and mix to a soft dough with your hands.

2 Turn out the dough on to a lightly floured surface and knead gently until smooth. Roll out the dough to 2cm/¾in thick with a rolling pin, then stamp out nine scones using a 6cm/ 2½in fluted cutter.

3 Place the scones on the prepared baking sheet and brush the tops with the remaining beaten egg. Sprinkle the rest of the cheese and the sesame seeds on top and bake for 15 minutes, until golden. Transfer to a wire rack and leave to cool. To serve split in half and spread with butter.

Try this

Use self-raising (self-rising) flour instead of wholemeal (whole-wheat) flour and baking powder, if you like. Rosemary, basil or thyme can be used in place of the sage.

Peach and Redcurrant Tartlets

Sharp-tasting redcurrants and sweet peaches make a winning combination in these simple, but very pretty little tartlets.

You will need

25g/1oz/2 tbsp butter, melted
16 × 15cm/6in squares of filo pastry
icing (confectioners') sugar,
    for dusting
redcurrant sprigs, to decorate

For the filling

150ml/¼ pint/⅔ cup double
    (heavy) cream
130g/4¼oz carton peach and
    mango fromage frais or yogurt
a few drops vanilla essence (extract)
15ml/1 tbsp icing (confectioners')
    sugar, sifted

For the topping

2 peaches
50g/2oz/½ cup redcurrants

Makes 4 ⊕⊕⊕

1 Preheat the oven to 190°C/375°F/ Gas 5. Use a little of the butter to grease four large bun tins (muffin pans) or individual tartlet tins. Brush the pastry squares with butter, stack them in fours, then place in the tins to make four pastry cases (pie shells).

2 Bake for 12–15 minutes, until golden. Cool the filo cases on a wire rack.

3 Make the filling. Whip the cream to soft peaks, then lightly fold in the fromage frais, vanilla essence and icing sugar. Share the filling among the pastry cases.

4 Slice the peaches thinly and fan them out on top of the filling, interspersing with a few redcurrants. Decorate with redcurrant sprigs and dust with icing sugar.

English Muffins

These favourites are perfect served warm, split open and spread with butter and jam or try them split and topped with ham and eggs for brunch.

You will need

450g/1lb/4 cups strong white bread
    flour, plus extra for dusting
vegetable oil, for greasing
7.5ml/1½ tsp salt
350–375ml/12–13fl oz/
    1½–1⅔ cups lukewarm milk
2.5ml/½ tsp caster (superfine) sugar
15g/½oz fresh yeast
15ml/1 tbsp melted butter or olive oil
rice flour or semolina, for dusting

Makes 9 🍴🍴

1 Generously flour a non-stick baking sheet. Very lightly grease a griddle. Sift the flour and salt together into a large bowl and make a well in the centre. Blend 150ml/¼ pint/⅔ cup of the lukewarm milk, sugar and yeast together. Stir in the remaining milk and butter or olive oil.

2 Add the yeast mixture to the well and beat for 4–5 minutes, until smooth and elastic. The dough will be soft, but it will just hold its shape. Cover with lightly oiled clear film (plastic wrap) and leave to rise in a warm place for 45–60 minutes, or until the dough has doubled in bulk.

3 Turn out the dough on a well-floured surface and knock back (punch down). Roll it out to about 1cm/½in thick. Using a floured 7.5cm/3in plain cutter, stamp out nine rounds. Dust the rounds with rice flour or semolina and place on the baking sheet. Cover and leave to rise in a warm place for 20–30 minutes.

4 Warm the griddle or a heavy frying pan over a medium heat. Carefully transfer the muffins, in batches, to the griddle or pan. Cook gently for about 7 minutes on each side, or until they are golden brown. Transfer the muffins to a wire rack to cool slightly. Serve warm.

Handy hint

Muffins should be cut around the outer edge only, using a sharp knife, and then torn apart. If toasting, toast the whole muffins first and then split them in half. If you'd like to serve the muffins warm, transfer them to a wire rack to cool slightly before serving.

Wrap-up Rhubarb Pie

This method can be used for all sorts of fruit and is really easy. It doesn't matter how rough the pie looks when it goes into the oven; it comes out looking fantastic.

You will need

350g/12oz shortcrust (unsweetened) pastry, thawed if frozen
1 egg yolk, beaten
25g/1oz/3 tbsp semolina
25g/1oz/¼ cup hazelnuts, coarsely chopped
30ml/2 tbsp golden granulated sugar

For the filling

450g/1lb rhubarb, cut into 2.5cm/ 1in pieces
75g/3oz/⅓ cup caster (superfine) sugar
1–2 pieces preserved stem ginger in syrup, drained and finely chopped

Serves 6 🍴🍴🍴

1 Preheat the oven to 200°C/400°F/ Gas 6. Roll out the pastry to a round 35cm/14in across. Lay it over the rolling pin and lift it on to a large baking sheet. Brush a little egg yolk all over the pastry. Sprinkle the semolina over the centre, leaving a wide rim all around.

2 Make the filling. Place the rhubarb pieces, caster sugar and chopped ginger in a large bowl and mix well.

Handy hint
Egg yolk glaze brushed on to pastry gives it an attractive golden sheen.

3 Pile the rhubarb mixture into the middle of the pastry. Fold the rim over so that it almost covers the filling.

4 Glaze the pastry rim with any remaining egg yolk and sprinkle the hazelnuts and golden sugar over. Bake for 30–35 minutes, or until the pastry is golden brown. Serve warm.

Crumpets

Home-made crumpets are less doughy and not so heavy as most supermarket versions.
Serve them lightly toasted, oozing with butter.

2 Heat the milk and water mixture, oil and sugar until lukewarm. Mix the yeast with 150ml/¼ pint/⅔ cup of the warm liquid. Add the yeast mixture and remaining liquid to the well in the flour and beat vigorously for 5 minutes, until smooth and elastic. Cover with lightly oiled clear film (plastic wrap) and leave to rise in a warm place for about 1½ hours, or until bubbly.

3 Dissolve the soda in the lukewarm water and stir into the batter. Re-cover and leave to rise for 30 minutes.

4 Place the cutters or crumpet rings on the griddle and warm over a medium heat. Fill the cutters or rings 1cm/½in deep with the batter. Cook over a low heat for 6–7 minutes. The tops should be dry, with a mass of tiny holes. Remove the cutters or rings and turn the crumpets over. Cook for 1–2 minutes, until golden. Repeat with the remaining batter. Serve warm.

You will need

vegetable oil, for greasing
225g/8oz/2 cups plain (all-purpose) flour
225g/8oz/2 cups strong white bread flour
10ml/2 tsp salt
600ml/1 pint/2½ cups milk and water mixed
30ml/2 tbsp sunflower oil
15ml/1 tbsp caster (superfine) sugar
15g/½oz fresh yeast
2.5ml/½ tsp bicarbonate of soda (baking soda)
120ml/4fl oz/½ cup lukewarm water

Makes about 20 🍴🍴🍴

1 Lightly grease a griddle pan or heavy frying pan and several 4 × 8cm/1½ × 3¼in plain pastry cutters or crumpet rings with a little vegetable oil. Sift both types of flour and the salt together into a large bowl and make a well in the centre with your fingers or a spoon.

Handy hint

If the characteristic bubbles do not form on the crumpets as they cook, add a little more water to the batter before cooking the next batch of crumpets.

Caramel Apples

Use different coloured apples to make this dessert more fun. The creamy caramel sauce is simple to make and really yummy – like hot toffee apples.

You will need

3 green eating apples, cored but not peeled
3 red eating apples, cored but not peeled
150g/5oz/¾ cup light brown sugar
2.5ml/½ tsp grated nutmeg
1.5ml/¼ tsp ground black pepper
25g/1oz/¼ cup walnut pieces
25g/1oz/scant ¼ cup sultanas (golden raisins)
50g/2oz/¼ cup butter or margarine, diced

For the caramel sauce

15ml/1 tbsp butter or margarine
120ml/4fl oz/½ cup whipping cream

Serves 6 🍴🍴🍴

1 Preheat the oven to 190°C/375°F/ Gas 5. Grease a baking tin (pan) just large enough to hold all the apples in one layer. With a small knife, cut at an angle to enlarge the core opening at the stem end of each apple to about 2.5cm/1in in diameter. (The opening should resemble a funnel in shape.) Arrange the apples in the prepared tin, stem end up.

2 In a small pan, combine 175ml/ 6fl oz/¾ cup water with the brown sugar, nutmeg and pepper. Bring the mixture to the boil, stirring constantly. Boil for 6 minutes. Combine the walnuts and sultanas. Spoon some of the walnut-sultana mixture into the opening in each apple. Top each apple with some of the diced butter.

Try this

Use firm red and gold pears, but cook them for 10 minutes longer.

3 Spoon the brown sugar sauce over and around the apples. Bake, basting occasionally with the sauce, for 45–50 minutes, until the apples are just tender. Transfer the apples to a serving dish, reserving the brown sugar sauce in the baking tin. Keep the apples warm.

4 For the caramel sauce, mix the butter, cream and saved brown sugar sauce in a pan. Bring to the boil, stirring occasionally, and simmer for about 2 minutes, until thickened. Let the sauce cool slightly before serving.

Blueberry Muffins

Light and fruity, these well-known American muffins are delicious at any time of day. Serve them warm for breakfast or brunch.

You will need

180g/6¼oz/generous 1½ cups plain (all-purpose) flour
60g/2¼oz/generous ¼ cup sugar
10ml/2 tsp baking powder
1.5ml/¼ tsp salt
2 eggs
50g/2oz/4 tbsp butter, melted
175ml/6fl oz/¾ cup milk
5ml/1 tsp vanilla essence (extract)
5ml/1 tsp grated lemon rind
175g/6oz/1½ cups fresh blueberries

Makes 12 🌀🌀

1 Preheat the oven to 200°C/400°F/ Gas 6. Grease a 12 cup muffin tin (pan) or arrange 12 paper cases on a baking sheet. Sift the flour, sugar, baking powder and salt into a bowl.

2 Whisk the eggs in another bowl. Add the melted butter, milk, vanilla and grated lemon rind and stir well. Make a well in the dry ingredients and pour in the egg mixture. With a large metal spoon, stir until the flour is just moistened, but not smooth.

Handy hint
If you want to serve these muffins for breakfast, prepare the dry ingredients the night before.

3 Add the blueberries to the muffin mixture and gently fold in, being careful not to crush the berries. Spoon the batter into the muffin tin or paper cases, leaving enough room for the muffins to rise.

4 Bake for 20–25 minutes, until the tops spring back when you touch them lightly. Leave the muffins in the tin, if using, for 5 minutes before turning out on to a wire rack to cool a little before serving.

Try this
Muffins are delicious with all kinds of different fruits. Try replacing the blueberries with the same weight of bilberries, blackcurrants, pitted cherries or fresh raspberries.

What a Peach

A simple, rich dessert that's quick and easy to make and tastes terrific. Serve it on its own or with some whipped cream or thick yogurt.

You will need

115g/4oz/⅔ cup raspberries
30ml/2 tbsp icing
   (confectioners') sugar
4 ripe peaches
120ml/8 tbsp mascarpone cheese
45ml/3 tbsp soft brown sugar

Serves 4 🦺🦺

Handy hint
As the cheese melts, the sugar might slip off, so have some extra handy to sprinkle over the top of the peaches.

1 Save a few of the raspberries for decoration. Put the rest in a blender with the icing sugar and process until smooth. Use a hand-held blender if you prefer, or push the raspberries through a sieve with a wooden spoon and then mix with the sugar.

2 Cut around each peach lengthways and twist the fruit. One half should come away, leaving the stone (pit) in the other. Scoop out the stone and arrange the halves on a grill (broiler) pan, cut sides up. Preheat the grill.

3 Put 15ml/1 tbsp of cheese in the centre of each peach. Sprinkle the sugar over the top and grill (broil) until the cheese and sugar have melted.

4 Share the raspberry sauce among four plates and top with the peaches. Decorate with raspberries.

Banana and Nut Buns

These mouthwatering buns can be served warm for breakfast. If they don't all disappear straight away, munch on them as a healthy mid-afternoon snack.

You will need

50g/2oz/¼ cup butter or margarine, plus extra for greasing

150g/5oz/1¼ cups plain (all-purpose) flour

7.5ml/1½ tsp baking powder

175g/6oz/generous ¾ cup caster (superfine) sugar

1 egg

5ml/1 tsp vanilla essence (extract)

3 medium bananas, mashed

50g/2oz/½ cup chopped pecans

75ml/2½fl oz/⅓ cup milk

Makes 8 🍌🍌

1 Preheat the oven to 190°C/ 375°F/Gas 5. Grease eight patty tins (muffin pans) with a little butter or margarine. Sift the flour and baking powder into a small bowl. Set aside.

Handy hint

If you are not sure whether the buns are cooked all the way through, insert a skewer or wooden cocktail stick (toothpick). If it comes out clean, without any batter on it, the buns are ready.

2 With an electric mixer, cream together the butter or margarine and the sugar. Add the egg and vanilla essence and beat until fluffy. Mix in the bananas.

3 Add the pecans. With the mixer on low speed, beat in portions of the flour mixture and the milk, adding them alternately.

4 Spoon the mixture into the prepared tins. Bake for 20–25 minutes. Remove from the oven and cool for 10 minutes on a wire rack.

Baked Bananas with Ice Cream

Hot baked bananas make the perfect partner for delicious vanilla ice cream topped with a toasted hazelnut sauce. A quick and easy dessert that looks as good as it tastes.

You will need

4 large bananas
15ml/1 tbsp lemon juice
8 scoops of vanilla ice cream

For the sauce

25g/1oz/2 tbsp unsalted
   (sweet) butter
50g/2oz/½ cup hazelnuts, toasted
   and coarsely chopped
45ml/3 tbsp golden (light
   corn) syrup
30ml/2 tbsp lemon juice

Serves 4 🍴🍴

1 Preheat the oven to 180°C/350°F/ Gas 4. Place the unpeeled bananas on a baking sheet and brush them with the lemon juice. Bake for about 20 minutes, until the skins are turning black and the flesh gives a little when the bananas are gently squeezed.

2 Meanwhile, make the sauce. Melt the butter in a small pan. Add the hazelnuts and cook over a low heat, stirring frequently, for 1 minute. Add the syrup and lemon juice and heat gently, stirring constantly with a wooden spoon, for 1 minute more.

3 To serve, slit each banana open with a knife and open out the skins. Transfer to serving plates and serve with scoops of ice cream. Pour the sauce over.

Raisin Bran Muffins

These fruity bran muffins are simple to make – impress your friends when they come to stay and serve the muffins freshly cooked for breakfast.

You will need

50g/2oz/¼ cup butter or margarine
75g/3oz/⅔ cup plain
   (all-purpose) flour
50g/2oz/½ cup wholemeal (whole-
   wheat) flour
7.5ml/1½ tsp bicarbonate of soda
   (baking soda)
pinch of salt
5ml/1 tsp ground cinnamon
25g/1oz/½ cup bran
75g/3oz/generous ½ cup raisins
50g/2oz/¼ cup dark brown sugar
50g/2oz/¼ cup granulated sugar
1 egg
250ml/8fl oz/1 cup buttermilk
juice of ½ lemon

Makes 15 🍴🍴

1 Preheat the oven to 200°C/ 400°F/Gas 6. Grease 15 muffin tins (pans). Alternatively, you can line the tins with paper cases or use paper cases on their own. For extra strength, place them in pairs, one inside the other. Place the butter or margarine in a pan and melt over a low heat. Remove from the heat and set aside.

2 Sift together the plain flour, wholemeal flour, salt, bicarbonate of soda, and cinnamon. In another bowl, mix the egg, buttermilk, lemon juice and melted butter or margarine.

3 Add the egg mixture to the dry ingredients and stir lightly and quickly until just moistened; do not mix until smooth. Then add the bran, raisins and sugars, and stir until thoroughly mixed.

4 Spoon the batter into the prepared muffin tins or paper cases, filling them almost to the top. Bake for 15–20 minutes, until golden. Transfer to a wire rack to cool. Serve the muffins warm or at room temperature.

Totally Tropical Fruit Salad

Passion fruit makes a superb dressing for any fruit, but really brings out the flavour of exotic varieties. You can easily double the recipe, then serve the rest for breakfast.

You will need

1 mango
1 papaya
2 kiwi fruit
coconut or vanilla ice cream, to serve

For the dressing

3 passion fruit
thinly pared rind and juice of 1 lime
5ml/1 tsp hazelnut or walnut oil
15ml/1 tbsp clear honey

Serves 6 🍷

Handy hint

Orange blossom or acacia honey would be perfect for the dressing.

1 Peel the mango, cut it into three slices and cut off any flesh still clinging to the stone (pit). Then cut the flesh into chunks and place it in a large bowl. Peel the papaya and cut it in half. Scoop out the seeds, then chop the flesh.

2 Cut both ends off each kiwi fruit, then stand them on a board. Using a small sharp knife, cut off the skin from top to bottom. Cut each kiwi fruit in half lengthways, then cut into thick slices. Combine all the fruit in the bowl with the mango.

3 Make the dressing. Cut each passion fruit in half and scoop the seeds out into a sieve set over a small bowl. Press the seeds well to extract all their juices. Lightly whisk the remaining dressing ingredients into the passion fruit juice, then pour the dressing over the fruit. Mix gently to combine. Leave to chill for 1 hour before serving with scoops of coconut or vanilla ice cream.

Snacks and Light Meals

Raspberry and Rose Petal Shortcakes

Rose-water-scented cream and fresh raspberries form the filling for this scrumptious dessert. To make a quick version, use bought cookies.

You will need

115g/4oz/½ cup unsalted (sweet) butter, softened
50g/2oz/¼ cup caster (superfine) sugar
½ vanilla pod (bean), split, seeds saved
115g/4oz/1 cup plain (all-purpose) flour, plus extra for dusting
50g/2oz/⅓ cup semolina
icing (confectioners') sugar, for dusting

For the filling

300ml/½ pint/1¼ cups double (heavy) cream
15ml/1 tbsp icing (confectioners') sugar
2.5ml/½ tsp rose-water
450g/1lb/2½ cups raspberries

For the decoration

12 miniature roses, unsprayed
6 fresh mint sprigs
1 egg white, beaten
caster (superfine) sugar, for dusting

Makes 6 🍴🍴🍴

1 Cream the butter, caster sugar and vanilla seeds in a bowl until the mixture is pale and fluffy. Sift the flour and semolina together, then gradually work the dry ingredients into the creamed mixture to make a biscuit (cookie) dough.

2 Gently knead the dough on a lightly floured surface until it is smooth. Roll it out quite thinly and prick it all over with a fork. Using a 7.5cm/3in fluted cutter, stamp out 12 rounds. Carefully place the rounds, spaced a little apart on a baking sheet and chill in the refrigerator for 30 minutes.

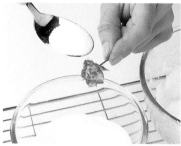

3 Meanwhile, make the filling. Put the cream and the icing sugar in a bowl and whisk until soft peaks form. Fold in the rose-water and chill until required. Preheat the oven to 180°C/350°F/Gas 4.

4 Bake the shortcakes for about 15 minutes, or until lightly golden. Lift them off the baking sheet with a metal spatula and cool on a wire rack.

5 To make the decoration, paint the roses and mint leaves with the egg white. Dust with caster sugar and place on a wire rack to dry.

6 To assemble the shortcakes, spoon the rose-water cream on to half the biscuits. Add a layer of raspberries, then top with a second shortcake. Dust with icing sugar. Decorate with the frosted roses and mint sprigs.

Veggie Soup

Easy to make as there's no need to be too fussy – just chop up lots of your favourite vegetables and simmer them gently with tomatoes and stock.

You will need

15ml/1 tbsp sunflower oil
1 onion, sliced
2 carrots, sliced
675g/1½lb potatoes, cut into
   large chunks
1.2 litres/2 pints/5 cups
   vegetable stock
450g/1lb can chopped tomatoes
115g/4oz broccoli, cut in florets
1 courgette (zucchini), sliced
115g/4oz/1½ cups mushrooms,
   thickly sliced
7.5ml/1½ tsp medium-hot curry
   powder (optional)
5ml/1 tsp dried mixed herbs
salt and ground black pepper
slices of fresh bread, to
   serve (optional)

Serves 4–6

2 Add the potatoes and cook gently for 2 minutes more. Stir them gently and regularly so that they do not stick to the pan. Pour in the stock, then add the chopped tomatoes, broccoli, courgette and mushrooms.

3 Stir in the curry powder (if using), with the herbs. Season lightly and bring to the boil. Cover and simmer gently for 30–40 minutes, or until the vegetables are tender. Serve hot with slices of fresh bread, if you like.

1 Heat the sunflower oil in a large pan, add the onion and carrots and cook over a low heat, stirring occasionally, for about 5 minutes, until they start to soften and the onions are just beginning to turn light brown.

Handy hint
For a special treat, serve this with breadsticks – they make handy edible stirrers.

Monster Meringues

A mouthwatering dessert made from meringue, whipped cream and tangy summer fruits. Chopped nectarines, peaches or melon also work well in this recipe.

You will need

3 egg whites
175g/6oz/generous ¾ cup caster (superfine) sugar
15ml/1 tbsp cornflour (cornstarch)
5ml/1 tsp white wine vinegar
few drops vanilla essence (extract)
225g/8oz assorted red summer fruits
300ml/½ pint/1¼ cups double (heavy) cream
1 passion fruit

Serves 4 🍴🍴🍴

Handy hint

Draw six 7.5cm/3in circles and pipe smaller meringues, if you aren't hungry enough for a monster dessert.

1 Preheat the oven to 140°C/275°F/ Gas 1. In pencil, draw eight 10cm/ 4in circles on two separate sheets of baking parchment paper which will fit on two flat baking sheets.

2 Whisk the egg whites until stiff. This will take about 2 minutes with an electric whisk. Add the sugar gradually and whisk well each time. The mixture should now be very stiff.

3 Use a metal spoon to gently stir in the cornflour, white wine vinegar and vanilla essence. Put the meringue into a large piping (pastry) bag, fitted with a large star nozzle. Pipe a solid layer of meringue in four of the circles and then pipe a lattice pattern in the other four. Cook for 1¼–1½ hours, swapping shelf positions after about 30 minutes, until lightly browned. The parchment will peel off easily when the meringues are cooked.

4 Chop most of the summer fruits, saving a few for decoration. Whip the cream and spread it over the solid meringues. Sprinkle the fruit over. Halve the passion fruit. Scoop out the seeds with a teaspoon and sprinkle them over the fruit. Add a lattice lid and serve with the saved fruits.

Carrot Soup

Carrots are said to improve your eyesight so this delicious soup is bound to help you to see in the dark. Serve this tasty lentil and carrot soup with toast or chunks of bread.

You will need

15ml/1 tbsp sunflower oil
1 onion, sliced
450g/1lb carrots, sliced
75g/3oz/scant ½ cup split red lentils
1.2 litres/2 pints/5 cups
   vegetable stock
5ml/1 tsp ground coriander
45ml/3 tbsp chopped fresh parsley
salt and ground black pepper

Serves 4 🍴🍴

Handy hint

Push the soup through a sieve with a wooden spoon or leave it chunky, if you don't have a food processor or blender.

1 Heat the oil, add the onion and cook until it is starting to brown. Add the sliced carrots and cook gently, stirring frequently, for about 4–5 minutes, until they start to soften. Meanwhile, put the lentils in a small bowl and cover with cold water. Pour off any bits that float on the surface. Tip the lentils into a sieve and rinse under cold running water.

2 Add the lentils, stock and coriander to the pan. Bring the soup to the boil. Lower the heat, cover and simmer gently for 30 minutes, or until the lentils are cooked and tender.

3 Add the parsley, salt and pepper and cook for 5 minutes. Set the pan aside to cool slightly.

4 Pour the soup into a blender or food processor and process until smooth. (You may have to do this a half at a time.) Rinse the pan and reheat the soup before serving.

Banana and Apricot Caramel Trifle

Everyone loves trifle, and ginger cake makes a delicious base in this version. You could use your favourite cake – try lemon, chocolate or orange, if you prefer.

You will need

300ml/½ pint/1¼ cups milk

4–5 drops vanilla essence (extract)

45ml/3 tbsp caster (superfine) sugar

20ml/4 tsp cornflour (cornstarch)

3 egg yolks

¼ packet apricot or tangerine jelly (flavoured gelatin)

60ml/4 tbsp apricot conserve

175–225g/6–8oz ginger cake, cut into cubes

3 bananas, sliced, with one saved for topping

90g/3½oz/½ cup granulated sugar

300ml/½ pint/1¼ cups double (heavy) cream, whipped

a few drops of lemon juice

Serves 6–8 🍴🍴

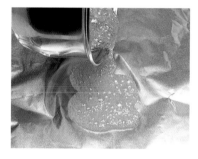

3 Put the jelly, apricot conserve and 60ml/4 tbsp water in a small pan and heat gently until all the jelly dissolves. Set aside until cool but not set. Put the cubed cake in a deep serving bowl or dish and pour on the jelly mixture. Cover with sliced bananas, then the custard. Chill for 1–2 hours.

4 Heat the sugar with 60ml/4 tbsp water and, when it has dissolved, boil until it is just golden. Immediately pour on to a sheet of foil, leave to harden, then break into pieces.

5 Spread the cream over the custard. Chill for 2 hours, then top with the sliced banana and the caramel pieces.

1 Pour the milk into a small pan. Add the vanilla essence to the milk and bring just to the boil, then remove the pan from the heat. Whisk together the sugar, cornflour and eggs until pale and creamy. Whisk in the milk and return the whole mixture to the pan. Heat to simmering point, stirring constantly, and cook gently over a low heat until the custard coats the back of a wooden spoon thickly.

2 Leave to cool, covered tightly with clear film (plastic wrap).

Chinese Soup

Take a tasty trip to the Far East, with this Chinese-style soup. It's based on the popular chicken and corn soup that is often served in Chinese restaurants.

You will need

15ml/1 tbsp sesame oil
4 spring onions (scallions),
    coarsely chopped
225g/8oz skinless chicken breast
    fillets, cut in small cubes
1.2 litres/2 pints/5 cups
    chicken stock
15ml/1 tbsp soy sauce
115g/4oz/1 cup frozen corn kernels
115g/4oz medium thread
    egg noodles
salt and ground black pepper
1 carrot, thinly sliced lengthways,
    to garnish
prawn crackers, to serve (optional)

Serves 4–6 🍴🍴

1 Heat the oil and cook the spring onions and chicken until the meat has browned all over.

2 Add the stock and the soy sauce and bring the soup to the boil.

3 Stir in the corn, then add the thread egg noodles, breaking them up coarsely. Taste the soup and add salt and pepper if needed. (Soy sauce is already quite salty.)

4 Use small cutters to stamp out shapes from the thin slices of carrot. Add them to the soup. Simmer for 5 minutes, before serving in bowls with prawn crackers, if you like.

Raspberry Trifle

A delicious dessert that you can make well in advance – use fresh raspberries in the summer when they are in season or frozen raspberries at other times of the year.

2 Save a few raspberries for decoration. Layer half the remaining raspberries on top of the cake.

3 Pour on half of the custard, covering all the fruit and the layer of cake. Repeat the layers. Cover and chill for at least 2 hours.

You will need

175g/6oz trifle sponges, halved and
   cut into 2.5cm/1in cubes, or plain
   sponge cake, cut into 2.5cm/
   1in cubes
40ml/2fl oz/¼ cup orange juice
115g/4oz/scant ½ cup raspberry jam
275g/10oz/1⅔ cups raspberries
450ml/¾ pint/scant 2 cups custard
300ml/½ pint/1¼ cups sweetened
   whipped cream
toasted sliced almonds and mint
   leaves, to decorate

Serves 6 🌡🌡

1 Arrange half of the trifle sponges or cake cubes evenly over the base of a large glass serving bowl. Sprinkle with half of the orange juice and spoon on half of the jam.

4 Just before serving, spoon the sweetened whipping cream evenly over the top. To decorate, sprinkle with toasted sliced almonds and arrange the saved raspberries and mint leaves on the top.

Potato Wedges

Much more interesting than ordinary baked potatoes, these wedges are served with a home-made spicy dip – they're great with tomato salsa too.

2 Scoop out some of the centre with a knife or spoon and put just the skins back in the roasting pan.

3 Brush the skins with a little oil and sprinkle with salt, then return to the oven. Cook for 30–40 minutes, until they are crisp and brown, brushing them occasionally with more oil.

You will need

8 large potatoes, scrubbed
30–45ml/2–3 tbsp oil
90ml/6 tbsp mayonnaise
30ml/2 tbsp natural (plain) yogurt
5ml/1 tsp curry paste
30ml/2 tbsp coarsely chopped fresh
    coriander (cilantro)
salt

Serves 4 🍴🍴

Handy hint
Leave the potatoes to cool slightly before cutting them into quarters.

1 Preheat the oven to 190°C/375°F/ Gas 5. Arrange the potatoes in a roasting pan, prick them all over with a fork and cook for 45 minutes, or until tender. Carefully cut each potato into quarters lengthways, holding it with a clean dishtowel if it's still a bit hot.

4 Stir the mayonnaise, yogurt, curry paste and 15ml/1 tbsp coriander in a small bowl. Put it in a clean bowl and sprinkle with the remaining coriander. Serve with the hot potato wedges.

Chocolate Puffs

These mini versions of chocolate eclairs are also known as profiteroles. They are always a firm favourite and easy to make.

You will need

150ml/¼ pint/⅔ cup water
50g/2oz/¼ cup butter
65g/2½oz/9 tbsp plain (all-purpose)
    flour, sifted
2 eggs, beaten

For the filling and icing

150ml/¼ pint/⅔ cup double
    (heavy) cream
225g/8oz/2 cups icing
    (confectioners') sugar
15ml/1 tbsp (unsweetened)
    cocoa powder)
30–60ml/2–4 tbsp water

Serves 4–6 🍷🍷🍷

1 Put the water in a pan, add the butter and heat gently until it melts. Bring to the boil and remove the pan from the heat. Tip in all the flour at once and beat quickly with a wooden spoon until the mixture sticks together, leaving the side of the pan clean. Leave to cool slightly.

2 Add the eggs, a little at a time, to the mixture and beat well each time, by hand with a wooden spoon or with an electric whisk, until the mixture is thick and glossy and drops reluctantly from a spoon (you may not need to use all of the egg). Preheat the oven to 220°C/425°F/Gas 7.

3 Dampen two baking sheets with cold water and put walnut-size spoonfuls of the mixture on them. Leave space for them to rise. Cook for 25–30 minutes, until they are golden brown and well risen. Use a spatula to lift them on to a wire rack and make a small hole in each one with the handle of a wooden spoon to allow the steam to escape. Leave to cool.

4 Make the filling and icing. Whip the cream until thick. Put it into a piping (pastry) bag fitted with a plain or star nozzle. Push the nozzle into the hole in each puff and squirt a little cream inside. Put the icing sugar and cocoa in a small bowl and stir together. Add enough water to make a thick glossy icing. Spread a spoonful of icing on each puff and serve.

Stuffed Mushrooms

Ideal for those vegetarians out there, this speedy snack is perfect on its own, on toast or with slices of fresh crusty bread.

You will need

50g/2oz/¼ cup butter

2 garlic cloves, peeled and crushed

4 large flat mushrooms, peeled or wiped

2.5cm/1in piece of fresh root ginger, grated

4 spring onions (scallions), cut in 2.5cm/1in pieces

1 carrot, cut in thin sticks

6 baby corn cobs, quartered lengthways

75g/3oz fine green beans, halved

30ml/2 tbsp soy sauce

115g/4oz/2 cups beansprouts, rinsed and drained

Serves 4 🍲🍲

2 Turn up the heat and add the ginger, spring onions, carrot, corn and beans to the pan and stir-fry for 2 minutes. (This means stirring and tossing the vegetables constantly.)

3 Add the soy sauce and the beansprouts and cook for 1 minute more. Put each mushroom on a plate and top with the stir-fried vegetables. Serve immediately.

1 Melt the butter in a large frying pan and cook the garlic until it has softened slightly. Add the mushrooms to the pan and cook over a low heat for 8–10 minutes, turning once or twice, until tender. Lift out the mushrooms, place in a dish and cover to keep them hot.

Handy hint

You should use a large pan for stir-frying so that the ingredients don't fly about all over the kitchen. A wok is ideal.

Chocolate Cups

Perfect for the chocoholics in the family, these impressive looking cups take a little effort but the results are well worthwhile. Serve with crisp dessert biscuits.

You will need
200g/7oz plain
 (semisweet) chocolate
120ml/4fl oz/½ cup double
 (heavy) cream
75g/3oz white chocolate

Serves 4 🍷🍷🍷

Handy hint
Try using white chocolate drops, chocolate-covered raisins or a chopped chocolate bar, instead of the white chocolate.

1 Break half the plain chocolate into pieces and put them in a bowl. Stand the bowl over a pan of hot, but not boiling, water and leave to melt, stirring occasionally. Make sure the water doesn't touch the bowl.

2 Line four ramekins or similarly sized cups with a piece of foil. Don't worry if it creases or scrunches up. Use a clean paintbrush to brush the melted chocolate over the foil in a thick layer. Chill in the refrigerator until set. Paint a second layer of chocolate and chill again.

3 Put the cream in a bowl and whisk until stiff. Melt the remaining plain chocolate as before and use a metal spoon to fold it into the cream. Coarsely chop the white chocolate and stir it gently into the chocolate and cream mixture.

4 Carefully peel the foil off the chocolate cups and fill each one with the chocolate and cream mixture. Chill until set. Serve immediately with your favourite dessert biscuits.

Stripy Mozzarella Slices

These colourful vegetable slices are made with several very popular and delicious Italian ingredients – tomatoes, fresh basil and mozzarella cheese.

You will need

45–60ml/3–4 tbsp olive oil,
   for brushing
1 large aubergine (eggplant)
1 large or 2 medium tomatoes,
   thickly sliced
a few fresh basil leaves, shredded
115g/4oz mozzarella cheese, sliced
salt and ground black pepper
fresh basil, to garnish

Serves 4 🍴🍴

1 Preheat the oven to 190°C/ 375°F/Gas 5. Brush a baking sheet with a little oil. Trim the aubergine and cut it lengthways into four slices about 5mm/¼in thick. Arrange the slices on the greased baking sheet.

Handy hint
Look for sun-ripened Italian plum tomatoes for the best flavour.

2 Brush the aubergine slices generously with the olive oil and sprinkle generously with the salt and ground black pepper.

3 Arrange about three or four tomato slices on top of each aubergine slice, overlapping them slightly, if necessary. Sprinkle over the shredded basil.

4 Interleave the cheese with the tomato. Brush with more oil. Bake for 15 minutes, then garnish with basil leaves and serve.

Chocolate Fudge Sundaes

They look impressive, taste fantastic and take only minutes to make. Serve the sundaes on a hot summer day – your friends will love them.

You will need

4 scoops each vanilla and coffee
 ice cream
2 small ripe bananas, sliced
whipped cream
toasted sliced almonds

For the sauce

50g/2oz/¼ cup light muscovado
 (brown) sugar
185g/6oz/½ cup golden syrup (light
 corn syrup)
45ml/3 tbsp strong black coffee
5ml/1 tsp ground cinnamon
150g/5oz plain (semisweet)
 chocolate, chopped
75ml/2½fl oz/⅓ cup whipping cream

Serves 4 🍶🍶🍶

2 Turn off the heat and stir in the chocolate. When it has melted and the sauce is smooth, stir in the cream. Let the sauce cool slightly. If made ahead, reheat it until just warm.

3 Fill four glasses with one scoop each of vanilla ice cream and coffee ice cream.

4 Arrange the sliced bananas over the scoops of ice cream, sharing them equally among the glasses. Pour the warm fudge sauce over the bananas, then top each sundae with a swirl of whipped cream. Sprinkle toasted, sliced almonds over the cream to decorate and serve the sundaes immediately.

1 To make the sauce, place the sugar, syrup, coffee and cinnamon in a large, heavy pan. Bring to a boil, then boil for about 5 minutes, stirring the mixture constantly.

Try this
Many variations are possible, using other flavours of ice cream such as strawberry, praline or chocolate. In the summer, substitute raspberries or strawberries for the bananas.

Egg-stuffed Tomatoes

This simple dish is just the kind of thing you might find in a family café in France. It is easy to make at home and makes a delicious after-school snack or a light lunch.

You will need

175ml/6fl oz/¾ cup mayonnaise
30ml/2 tbsp chopped fresh chives
30ml/2 tbsp chopped fresh basil
30ml/2 tbsp chopped fresh parsley
4 hard-boiled eggs, shelled
4 ripe tomatoes
salt and ground black pepper
salad leaves, to serve

Serves 4 🍴

1 Mix together the mayonnaise and herbs. Set aside. With an egg slicer or sharp knife, cut the eggs into thin slices, taking care to keep them intact.

2 Using a very sharp knife, make deep cuts to within 1cm/½ in of the base of each tomato. (There should be the same number of cuts in each tomato as there are slices of hard-boiled egg.)

3 Fan open the tomatoes and sprinkle with salt, then insert an egg slice into each slit. Place each tomato on a plate with a few salad leaves, season with salt and pepper and serve with the herb mayonnaise.

Ice Cream Bombes

This chilly dessert with warm sauce will have you ready to explode – it's dynamite. The ice cream needs to set overnight so remember to make it the day before you need it.

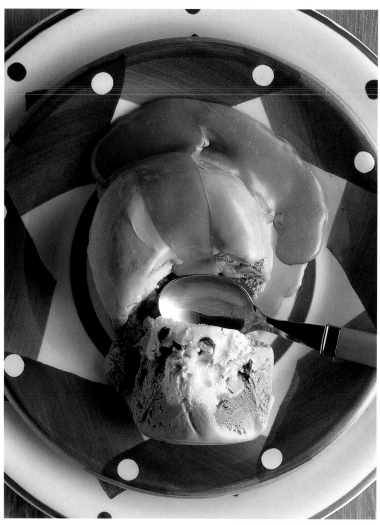

2 Put the vanilla ice cream in a small bowl and break it up slightly with a spoon. Stir in the chocolate drops and then spoon it into the dips in the chocolate ice cream. Return the cups to the freezer and leave overnight.

3 Put the toffees in a pan and heat gently, stirring. As they melt, add the cream and keep stirring until all the toffees have melted.

4 Dip the cups in hot water and run a knife around the edge. Turn out and pour the warm sauce over the top.

You will need

1 litre/1¾ pints/4 cups soft-scoop
  chocolate ice cream
475ml/16fl oz/2 cups soft-scoop
  vanilla ice cream
50g/2oz/⅓ cup plain (semisweet)
  chocolate drops
115g/4oz toffees (taffies)
75ml/5 tbsp double (heavy) cream

Serves 6

1 Share the chocolate ice cream among six small cups. Push it down to the base and up the sides, leaving a small, cup-shaped dip in the middle. Don't worry if it's not very neat; it will be frozen again before the ice cream melts too much. Place the cups in the freezer and leave for at least 45 minutes. Take them out again and smooth the ice cream into shape. Return to the freezer.

Tasty Toasts

Next time friends come over to watch a video, surprise them with these fabulous, home-made toasts — so much more impressive than calling out for pizza.

2 Put the oil in a small bowl and stir in the garlic. Cut the bread into slanting slices and brush one side with the garlic-flavoured oil. Place under a hot grill until browned.

3 Turn the slices over and brush the untoasted sides with the garlic-flavoured oil and pesto.

You will need

2 red (bell) peppers, halved
  lengthways and seeded
30ml/2 tbsp oil
1 garlic clove, peeled and crushed
1 French baton (short French stick)
45ml/3 tbsp pesto
50g/2oz/⅓ cup soft French
  goat's cheese

Serves 4 🍴🍴

Handy hint
Use cooking tongs to handle the charred peppers.

1 Put the pepper halves, cut side down, under a hot grill (broiler) and let the skins blacken. Carefully put the halves in a plastic bag, tie the top and leave them until they are cool enough to handle. Peel off the skins and cut the peppers into strips.

4 Arrange pepper strips over each slice and put small wedges of goat's cheese on top. Put back under the grill and toast until the cheese has browned and melted slightly.

Banana and Toffee Ice Cream

A really yummy combination of bananas and creamy toffees are used to make this great ice cream. Top with chocolate sauce and chopped nuts for a special treat.

You will need

3 ripe bananas
juice of 1 lemon
370g/12½oz can sweetened
   condensed milk
150ml/¼ pint/⅔ cup whipping cream
150g/5oz toffees (taffies)
chopped toffees (taffies),
   to decorate

Serves 4–6 🍨🍨🍨

1 Put the peeled bananas in a food processor or blender and process until smooth, then add the lemon juice and process briefly to mix. Scrape the purée into a plastic tub or a similar freezerproof container.

2 Pour in the condensed milk, stirring with a metal spoon, then add the cream. Mix well, cover and freeze for 4 hours, or until mushy.

Handy hint
Because of the consistency of the sweetened condensed milk this ice cream takes a long time to freeze. To reduce the first freezing time, start chilling the mixture in a roasting pan, transferring to a plastic tub only after adding the toffees (taffies).

3 Unwrap the toffees and chop them finely, using a very sharp knife. Be extremely careful as the knife can slip easily. If this proves difficult, put them in a plastic bag, then put that bag in another plastic bag for extra strength, tie the top and hit the toffees with a rolling pin.

4 Beat the semi-frozen ice cream with a fork or electric mixer to break up the ice crystals, then stir in the toffees. Return the ice cream to the freezer for 3–5 hours, or until firm. Scoop on to a plate or into a bowl and decorate with chopped toffees. Serve immediately.

Elegant Egg Sandwiches

A well-made egg sandwich is one of the best and quickest after-school snacks. Here are two favourite fillings, delicious at any time of day.

You will need

12 thin slices white or brown bread
50g/2oz/¼ cup butter, at
    room temperature
slices of lemon, to garnish

For the egg and cress filling

2 small (US medium) hard-boiled
    eggs, shelled and finely chopped
30ml/2 tbsp mayonnaise
½ carton cress
salt and ground black pepper

For the egg and tuna filling

2 small (US medium) hard-boiled
    eggs, shelled and finely chopped
25g/1oz canned tuna in oil, drained
    and mashed
5ml/1 tsp paprika
squeeze of lemon juice
25g/1oz piece cucumber, peeled and
    thinly sliced

Serves 6 🍴

2 To make the egg and cress filling, mix the chopped eggs with the mayonnaise, cress and a little salt and pepper. Layer between six slices of bread. Press down gently and cut into neat triangles.

3 To make the egg and tuna filling, mix the chopped eggs with the tuna, paprika, lemon juice, salt and pepper. Put cucumber on three slices of bread, top with the tuna mixture and the rest of the bread. Press down lightly and cut each sandwich into three neat rectangles.

4 Arrange all the sandwiches on a plate and garnish with lemon slices. Serve immediately. Alternatively, cover with damp kitchen paper, then wrap tightly in clear film (plastic wrap) and chill until required. The sandwiches should keep fresh for 2–3 hours.

1 Carefully trim the crusts off the bread, using a sharp, serrated knife, then spread the bread thinly and evenly with soft butter.

Try this

Use a combination of white and brown bread.

Simple Strawberry Ice Cream

Home-made ice cream is a real treat – this easy recipe is a delicious combination of strawberries and cream. Serve it with a few fresh strawberries as decoration.

You will need

500g/1¼lb/5 cups
   strawberries, hulled
50g/2oz/½ cup icing
   (confectioners') sugar
juice of ½ lemon
300ml/½ pint/1¼ cups
   whipping cream
extra strawberries, to decorate

Serves 4–6 🕐🕐

Handy hint

Buy strawberries in the summer when they are in season. Imported ones are not so nice.

1 Place the strawberries in a food processor or blender and process until smooth, then add the icing sugar and lemon juice and process again to mix. Scrape the purée into a sieve set over a bowl and press it through. Throw away the seeds left in the sieve. Chill the purée until very cold.

2 Whip the cream until it is just thickened but still falls from a spoon. Fold it into the purée, then pour into a plastic tub or a similar freezerproof container. Freeze for 6 hours until firm, beating twice with a fork, electric whisk or in a food processor to break up the ice crystals.

Ciabatta Sandwich

If you can find a ciabatta flavoured with sun-dried tomatoes, it makes the sandwich even tastier. Prosciutto is the Italian name for Parma ham.

You will need

60ml/4 tbsp mayonnaise
30ml/2 tbsp pesto
1 ciabatta loaf
115g/4oz provolone or mozzarella cheese, sliced
75g/3oz prosciutto, thinly sliced
4 plum tomatoes, sliced
fresh basil sprigs, torn into pieces

Makes 3 ⓦ

1 Stir together the mayonnaise and pesto in a small bowl until they are thoroughly mixed.

2 Cut the ciabatta in half horizontally with a sharp, serrated knife and spread the cut side of both halves with the pesto mayonnaise. Lay the cheese over one half of the ciabatta.

3 Cut the prosciutto into strips and arrange over the top. Cover with the sliced tomatoes and torn basil leaves. Sandwich together with the other half and cut into three pieces.

Chunky Choc Ice Cream

The three different chocolates in this rather grown-up ice cream make it so more-ish that it will rapidly disappear unless you hide it at the back of the freezer.

You will need

4 egg yolks
75g/3oz/6 tbsp caster
   (superfine) sugar
5ml/1 tsp cornflour (cornstarch)
300ml/½ pint/1¼ cups milk
200g/7oz milk chocolate
50g/2oz dark (bittersweet) chocolate,
   plus extra to decorate
50g/2oz white chocolate
300ml/½ pint/1¼ cups
   whipping cream

Serves 4–6 🍴🍴🍴

1 Whisk together the egg yolks, caster sugar and cornflour in a bowl until the mixture is thick and foamy. Pour the milk into a large, heavy pan. Heat the milk and bring it just to the boil, then gradually pour it on to the egg yolk mixture, whisking constantly. Return the custard mixture to the pan and cook over a low heat, stirring constantly with a wooden spoon until the custard thickens and is smooth. It should coat the back of the spoon.

2 Pour the custard back into the bowl. Break 150g/5oz of the milk chocolate into squares, stir these into the hot custard, then cover with clear film (plastic wrap). Leave to cool, then chill. Chop the remaining milk, dark and white chocolate finely.

3 Whip the cream until it has thickened but is still soft enough to fall from a spoon. Fold the whipped cream into the custard, pour into a plastic tub or a similar freezerproof container and freeze for 4 hours, beating once with a fork, electric whisk or in a food processor.

Handy hint

For maximum flavour, use good quality chocolate or your favourite chocolate bar. Don't use dark, milk or white cake covering because they aren't rich enough.

4 Beat the ice cream one more time. Fold in the pieces of chocolate and freeze for at least 2–3 hours, or until the ice cream is firm enough to scoop. Serve in glass dishes, decorated with the extra dark chocolate.

Frankfurter and Potato Salad Sandwich

An unlikely mixture to put into a sandwich, but one that works extremely well. If the potato salad is a bit too chunky, chop it a little first.

You will need

115g/4oz/⅔ cup potato salad
2 spring onions (scallions), chopped
25g/1oz/2 tbsp softened butter
4 slices wholemeal (whole-
   wheat) bread
4 frankfurters
2 tomatoes, sliced

Makes 2 🍴

1 Mix the potato salad with the spring onions in a bowl.

2 Butter the bread and share the potato salad equally between two slices, spreading it to the edges.

Try this
Shell and chop 1 hard-boiled egg and mix with 15ml/1 tbsp mayonnaise and 15ml/1 tbsp chopped fresh chives.

3 Slice the frankfurters diagonally and arrange them over the potato salad with the tomato slices.

4 Sandwich with the remaining bread, press together lightly and then cut in half diagonally.

Pineapple Sorbet on Sticks

So much better than store-bought ices and great fun to make, too. Fresh pineapple has a deliciously sweet flavour and is ideal for refreshing you on a hot day.

2 Heat the sugar and water in a heavy pan, stirring frequently until the sugar dissolves. Bring to the boil and boil for 3 minutes, without stirring, to make a syrup. Remove the pan from the heat and leave to cool.

3 Stir the lime juice and pineapple juice into the syrup, then chill until very cold. Pour the mixture into a container suitable for the freezer and freeze for 3–4 hours, beating twice as it thickens.

You will need

1 medium pineapple, about
   1.2kg/2½lb
115g/4oz/½ cup caster
   (superfine) sugar
300ml/½ pint/1¼ cups water
30ml/2 tbsp lime juice

Makes about 12 🍦🍦🍦

4 Spoon the mixture into 12 ice lolly (popsicle) moulds. Press a wooden lolly stick into the centre of each sorbet (sherbet). Freeze overnight until firm.

Handy hint

To make pink lollies, use 3 pink grapefruit instead of the pineapple. Peel and slice the grapefruit and blend them in a food processor. Add orange juice instead of lime juice.

1 Slice off the pineapple top and base, then cut away all the skin. Cut the pineapple in half lengthways and cut away the core in the middle. Coarsely chop the flesh, place it in a food processor and process until smooth. Press the pulp through a sieve placed over a bowl to extract as much juice as possible.

5 To serve the lollies, dip the moulds in very hot water for 1–2 seconds, but do not let the water come over the top, then carefully pull each lolly from the mould.

Classic BLT

This delicious American sandwich is made with crispy fried bacon, lettuce and tomato. Choose the bread you prefer and toast it if you like.

You will need

4 slices Granary (multigrain) bread
15g/½oz/1 tbsp softened butter
few crisp lettuce leaves, such as
   Cos, Romaine or Iceberg
1 large tomato, sliced
8 bacon rashers (strips)
30ml/2 tbsp mayonnaise

Makes 2 🍴🍴

1 Spread two of the slices of bread with butter. Lay the lettuce over the bread and cover with sliced tomato.

2 Grill (broil) the bacon under a medium heat until it just begins to crisp, then arrange it on top of the sliced tomato.

3 Spread the remaining slices of bread with mayonnaise. Lay them over the bacon, press the sandwich together gently and cut in half.

Raspberry Granita

This brilliant bright red, slushy ice looks spectacular. For a really fabulous dessert, serve it with whole berries and cream, Knickerbocker Glory style.

You will need

115g/4oz/½ cup caster
   (superfine) sugar
300ml/½ pint/1¼ cups water
500g/1¼lb/3⅓ cups raspberries,
   hulled, plus extra to decorate
juice of 1 lemon
little sifted icing (confectioners')
   sugar, for dusting

Serves 6 ⑪⑪⑪

1 Tip the caster sugar and water into a large pan and bring to the boil, stirring frequently until the sugar has completely dissolved. Pour the sugar syrup into a heatproof bowl, leave to cool, then chill in the refrigerator.

2 Put the raspberries in a food processor and process until smooth. Alternatively, put them in batches in a blender and process until smooth. Spoon the raspberry purée into a fine sieve set over a large bowl. Press the purée through the sieve with the back of the spoon and then discard the seeds left in the sieve.

3 Scrape the raspberry purée into a large measuring jug (cup), stir in the sugar syrup and lemon juice until thoroughly mixed. Top up the mixture with cold water to make 1 litre/1¾ pints/4 cups.

4 Pour the mixture into a large plastic container, suitable for the freezer, so that the depth is no more than 2.5cm/1in. Cover with a lid or a double thickness of foil and place in the freezer for about 2 hours, until the mixture around the sides of the container is beginning to freeze and has become mushy.

5 Remove the container from the freezer and, using a fork, break up the ice crystals around the sides and mash the mixture finely. Spread out the mixture evenly again, cover the container and return to the freezer for 30 minutes.

6 Beat the mixture and freeze again for 30 minutes three more times, until the ice forms fine, even crystals.

7 Spoon into tall glass dishes and decorate with extra raspberries dusted with a little sifted icing sugar.

Tuna and Corn Bap

Tuna and corn make a delicious combination. The filling is rather soft, so it is better served in a roll, which is firmer to hold, than between slices of bread.

You will need

90g/3½oz canned tuna, drained
90ml/6 tbsp cooked corn kernels
60ml/4 tbsp chopped cucumber
2 spring onions (scallions), chopped
90ml/6 tbsp tartare sauce
2 Granary (multigrain) baps (rolls)
2 green or lollo rosso lettuce leaves

Makes 2 🍴

Tartare Sauce

Mix 90ml/6 tbsp mayonnaise with 10ml/2 tsp each chopped gherkins, capers and parsley.

1 Flake the tuna and mix it with the corn, cucumber, spring onions and 30ml/2 tbsp of the tartare sauce.

3 Place a lettuce leaf on top of the tuna filling, cover with the remaining tartare sauce and replace the top of each bap.

2 Cut the baps in half crossways and share the filling between the bottom halves.

Desserts and Drinks

Egg and Bacon Caesar Salad

Quail's eggs give this salad an air of luxury, but you can use 4–6 hen's eggs instead, if you like.

You will need

3 × 1cm/½in thick slices white bread
45ml/3 tbsp olive oil
1 large garlic clove, finely chopped
3–4 Little Gem (Bibb) lettuces or
    2 larger cos or romaine lettuces
12–18 quail's eggs
115g/4oz thinly sliced prosciutto
40–50g/1½–2oz/½–⅔ cup grated
    Parmesan cheese
salt and ground black pepper

For the dressing

1 large (US extra large) egg
1–2 garlic cloves, chopped
4 anchovy fillets in oil, drained
120ml/4fl oz/½ cup olive oil
10–15ml/2–3 tsp lemon juice

Serves 4 🐟🐟🐟

1 Preheat the oven to 190°C/375°F/ Gas 5. Cut the bread into bitesize chunks and place them in a bowl with the oil and garlic. Toss them well with a wooden spoon to coat all over. Season with salt and pepper. Spread them out on a baking sheet. Bake for 10–14 minutes, stirring once or twice, until brown all over. Remove the baking sheet from the oven and set aside.

2 To make the dressing, bring a pan of water to the boil and add the egg. Boil it for 90 seconds. Place the egg in cold water to stop it cooking any more. Remove the shell, then place in a food processor. Add the garlic and anchovy fillets and process to mix. With the motor still running, gradually add the olive oil in a thin stream. Add the lemon juice and season to taste with salt and pepper.

3 Trim the lettuces, cutting the small lettuces into quarters or separating the larger lettuces into leaves. Place them in a large salad bowl.

4 Place the quail's eggs in a pan, cover with cold water, then bring to the boil and boil for 2 minutes. Place the eggs in cold water to stop them cooking any more, then part-shell them. Grill (broil) the prosciutto under a medium heat for 2–3 minutes on each side, or until crisp.

5 Toss the dressing into the lettuce with 25g/1oz of the Parmesan cheese. Add the bread cubes. Halve the quail's eggs and add them to the salad. Crumble the ham into large pieces and sprinkle it over the salad with the remaining cheese. Serve immediately.

Lamb Kebabs

Kebabs are popular all over the world – in this recipe, lean lamb is marinated, then cooked with chunks of vegetables to produce a delicious, colourful meal.

You will need

675g/1½lb lean lamb, cut into
    4cm/1½in cubes
12 baby (pearl) onions
2 green (bell) peppers, seeded and
    cut into 12 pieces
12 cherry tomatoes
12 button (white) mushrooms
lemon slices and fresh rosemary
    sprigs, to garnish
freshly cooked rice and crusty bread,
    to serve

For the marinade

juice of 1 lemon
120ml/4fl oz/½ cup orange juice
1 onion, finely chopped
60ml/4 tbsp olive oil
2.5ml/½ tsp dried sage
2.5ml/½ tsp chopped fresh rosemary
salt and ground black pepper

Serves 6 🍴🍴

1 To make the marinade, mix together the lemon and orange juice, onion, olive oil, herbs, salt and pepper in a bowl. Stir the cubes of lamb into the marinade. Cover with clear film (plastic wrap) and chill in the refrigerator for 2–12 hours, stirring occasionally.

Handy hint

If you are using wooden skewers, before you start cooking, you should soak the skewers in cold water for about 30 minutes. This will prevent them from burning during grilling (broiling).

2 Remove the lamb pieces from the marinade and thread on to six skewers with the onions, peppers, tomatoes and mushrooms. Preheat the grill (broiler).

3 Brush the kebabs with marinade and grill (broil) for 10–15 minutes, turning once. Arrange on cooked rice, with lemon and rosemary. Serve with crusty bread.

Warm Chicken and Tomato Salad

This simple, warm salad combines pan-fried chicken and spinach with a light, nutty dressing. Make it for lunch for the whole family on an autumn day.

You will need

45ml/3 tbsp olive oil
30ml/2 tbsp hazelnut oil
15ml/1 tbsp white wine vinegar
1 garlic clove, crushed
15ml/1 tbsp chopped fresh
    mixed herbs
225g/8oz baby spinach leaves
250g/9oz cherry tomatoes, halved
1 bunch spring onions
    (scallions), chopped
2 skinless, boneless chicken
    breast portions, cut into
    thin strips
salt and ground black pepper

Serves 4 🍴🍴

1 First make the dressing: place 30ml/2 tbsp of the olive oil, the hazelnut oil, vinegar, garlic and chopped herbs in a small bowl or jug (pitcher) and whisk together until thoroughly mixed. Set aside.

2 Trim any long stalks from the spinach leaves, then place in a large serving bowl with the tomatoes and spring onions, and toss together.

3 Heat the remaining olive oil in a frying pan and stir-fry the chicken over a high heat for 7–10 minutes, until it is cooked, tender and lightly browned all over.

4 Arrange the cooked chicken pieces over the salad. Whisk the dressing to blend, then drizzle it over the salad. Add salt and pepper to taste, toss lightly and serve immediately.

Nutty Chicken Kebabs

A tasty treat from Thailand that's quick to make and uses peanut butter – everyone's favourite spread – in the dip.

You will need

30ml/2 tbsp oil
15ml/1 tbsp lemon juice
450g/1lb skinless chicken breast
 fillets, cut in small cubes
sliced cucumber and lemon wedges,
 to serve

For the dip

5ml/1 tsp chilli powder
75ml/5 tbsp water
15ml/1 tbsp oil
1 small onion, grated
1 garlic clove, peeled and crushed
30ml/2 tbsp lemon juice
60ml/4 tbsp crunchy peanut butter
5ml/1 tsp salt
5ml/1 tsp ground coriander

Serves 4 🦃🦃

1 Mix the oil and lemon juice together in a glass or china bowl and add the cubed chicken. Cover with clear film (plastic wrap) and leave to marinate for at least 30 minutes.

2 Soak 12 wooden skewers in cold water for about 30 minutes to prevent them from burning during grilling (broiling).

3 Thread four or five cubes on each wooden skewer. Cook under a hot grill (broiler), turning frequently, for about 10 minutes, until cooked and browned. Cut one piece open to check it is cooked right through: this is very important with chicken.

4 Meanwhile, make the dip. Mix the chilli powder with 15ml/1 tbsp of the water. Heat the oil in a small frying pan, add the onion and garlic and cook for about 5 minutes, until tender.

5 Turn down the heat. Add the chilli paste and the remaining ingredients and stir well. Stir in more water if the sauce is too thick and put it into a small bowl. Serve warm, with the chicken kebabs, cucumber slices and lemon wedges.

Salad Niçoise

Made with the freshest of ingredients, this popular French salad makes a simple yet unbeatable summer dish. Serve with country-style bread or a crisp baguette.

3 Mix together the salad leaves, sliced cucumber, tomatoes and green beans in a large, shallow bowl. Halve the anchovies lengthways and shell and cut the eggs in quarters.

4 Preheat the grill (broiler). Brush the tuna steak with olive oil and sprinkle with salt and black pepper. Grill (broil) for 3–4 minutes on each side, until cooked through. Leave to cool, then flake with a fork.

You will need

115g/4oz green beans, trimmed and cut in half
115g/4oz mixed salad leaves
½ small cucumber, thinly sliced
4 ripe tomatoes, cut in quarters
50g/2oz can anchovies in olive oil, drained
4 eggs, hard-boiled
1 tuna steak, about 175g/6oz
olive oil, for brushing
½ bunch small radishes, trimmed
50g/2oz/½ cup small black olives
salt and ground black pepper

For the dressing

90ml/6 tbsp extra virgin olive oil
2 garlic cloves, crushed
15ml/1 tbsp white wine vinegar

Serves 4 🍴🍴

1 To make the dressing, whisk together the oil, garlic and vinegar and season to taste with salt and pepper. Set aside. Alternatively, put the oil, garlic and vinegar in a screw-top jar, secure the lid and shake well to mix, then add salt and pepper.

2 Cook the green beans in a pan of boiling water for 2 minutes, until just tender, then drain.

5 Sprinkle the flaked tuna, halved anchovies, quartered eggs, radishes and olives over the salad. Pour over the dressing and toss together lightly. Serve immediately.

Try this

If you like, you can include a few tiny, cooked new potatoes in the salad.

Homeburgers

These look the same as ordinary burgers, but watch out for the soft, cheesy centre.
Serve with fries and sliced tomatoes.

You will need

450g/1lb lean minced (ground) beef
2 slices of bread, crusts removed
1 egg
4 spring onions (scallions),
   coarsely chopped
1 garlic clove, peeled and chopped
15ml/1 tbsp mango chutney
10ml/2 tsp dried mixed herbs
50g/2oz mozzarella cheese
salt and ground black pepper
4 burger buns, to serve

Serves 4 🍴🍴

3 Cut the mozzarella into four equal pieces and put one piece in the centre of each piece of beef. Wrap the meat round the cheese to make a thick burger, covering the cheese completely. Chill for about 30 minutes. Preheat the grill (broiler).

4 Put the burgers on a rack under the hot grill, but not too close or they will burn on the outside before the middle has cooked properly. Cook them for 5–8 minutes on each side, then put each burger in a roll, with your favourite trimmings.

1 Put the beef, bread, egg, spring onions and garlic in a food processor. Add a little salt and pepper and process until evenly blended. Add the mango chutney and mixed herbs and process again.

2 Divide the mixture into four equal portions and pat flat, with damp hands to stop the meat from sticking.

Tuna and Tomato Salad

This salad is a posh version of the classic salad Niçoise and uses fresh tuna steaks, with green beans, cherry tomatoes and a herb and spice marinade.

You will need

6 tuna steaks
450g/1lb/3 cups green beans
450g/1lb/3 cups broad (fava) beans
1 cos or romaine lettuce
450g/1lb cherry tomatoes, halved
30ml/2 tbsp coarsely chopped fresh
    coriander (cilantro)
3 hard-boiled eggs
45ml/3 tbsp extra virgin olive oil
10–15ml/2–3 tsp lime or lemon juice
½ garlic clove, crushed
175g/6oz/1½ cups black olives

For the marinade

1 onion, cut into quarters
2 garlic cloves, halved
½ bunch fresh parsley
½ bunch fresh coriander (cilantro)
10ml/2 tsp paprika
45ml/3 tbsp olive oil
30ml/2 tbsp white wine vinegar
15ml/1 tbsp lime or lemon juice
45ml/3 tbsp water

Serves 6 🐟🐟🐟

2 Cook the green beans and broad beans in boiling salted water for 5–10 minutes, or until tender. Drain, rinse in cold running water and drain again. Remove the outer shells from the broad beans and place the beans in a large serving bowl with the green beans. Remove the outer leaves from the lettuce and tear the inner leaves into pieces. Add to the bowl with the tomatoes and coriander.

3 Shell the eggs and cut into eighths with a sharp knife. To make the dressing, whisk the olive oil, lime or lemon juice and garlic in a bowl.

4 Preheat the grill (broiler) and arrange the fish steaks on a grill pan. Brush with the marinade mixed with a little olive oil and grill for 5–6 minutes on each side.

5 Leave the fish to cool a little and then break the steaks into large pieces. Toss into the salad with the olives and dressing. Add the eggs and serve immediately.

Handy hint

If you are in a rush, then you can cut the marinating time down to 20 minutes.

1 Put all the marinade ingredients in a food processor and process for 40 seconds. Prick the tuna all over with a fork, place in a shallow dish in one layer and add the marinade. Turn the fish so that each piece is coated. Cover with clear film (plastic wrap) and leave in a cool place for 2 hours.

Snacks and Light Meals

Bean Burgers

Although these take a little time and effort to make, they are a delicious alternative to store-bought veggie burgers. Serve in buns with your favourite relish.

3 Shape the rice and bean mixture into 12 patties, using wet hands if the mixture sticks. Coat the patties in wholemeal flour and set aside.

4 Heat the vegetable oil in a large frying pan. Cook the burgers, in batches, until browned on each side. This will take about 5 minutes in total. Remove and drain on kitchen paper. Serve in buns with salad and relish.

You will need

200g/7oz/1 cup long grain brown rice
30ml/2 tbsp sunflower oil
50g/2oz/¼ cup butter
1 onion, chopped
2 garlic cloves, crushed
1 small green (bell) pepper, seeded and chopped
1 carrot, coarsely grated
400g/14oz can aduki beans, drained
1 egg, beaten
115g/4oz/1 cup grated Cheddar cheese
5ml/1 tsp dried thyme
50g/2oz/½ cup roasted hazelnuts
salt and ground black pepper
wholemeal (whole-wheat) flour, for coating
30ml/2 tbsp vegetable oil
buns, salad and relish, to serve

Serves 6 🍷🍷

1 Cook the rice in a large pan of boiling water for about 40 minutes, until it is very soft. Drain the rice and transfer it to a large bowl.

2 Heat the oil and butter in a frying pan, add the onion, garlic, green pepper and carrot and cook for about 10 minutes, until softened. Tip the mixture into the rice, together with the aduki beans, egg, cheese, thyme and nuts. Season lightly with salt and pepper, then chill until quite firm.

Handy hint

Aduki – or, sometimes, adzuki – beans are small, red and shiny with quite a sweet flavour. You could use other canned beans for these burgers if you like. Try red kidney beans or even Italian borlotti beans. When using canned beans, drain them well, then rinse under cold running water and drain well again.

Mozzarella and Avocado Salad

This colourful salad is an Italian favourite and it's very easy to make. Serve it with fresh bread, preferably warm ciabatta slices.

You will need

150g/5oz mozzarella cheese, thinly sliced

4 large plum tomatoes, sliced

sea salt flakes, to season

1 large avocado

about 12 fresh basil leaves or a small handful of fresh flat leaf parsley leaves

45–60ml/3–4 tbsp extra virgin olive oil

ground black pepper

Serves 2 🅥

1 Arrange the cheese and tomatoes on two salad plates. Crush over a pinch of sea salt flakes. Set aside in a cool place to marinate for 30 minutes.

2 Just before serving, cut the avocado in half using a large sharp knife and twist to separate. Lift out the stone (pit) and remove the peel.

3 Slice the avocado flesh crossways into half moons, or cut it into large chunks if that is easier.

4 Place the avocado on the salad, then sprinkle with the basil or parsley. Drizzle over the olive oil, add a little more salt and some black pepper. Serve at room temperature, with chunks of crusty Italian ciabatta bread.

French Bread Pizzas

Crunchy French bread makes a great pizza base for party snacks. You could even serve these with a green salad or a tomato and basil salad for a simple meal.

You will need

2 small baguettes
175/6fl oz/¾ cup ready-made
    tomato sauce
75g/3oz sliced cooked ham
4 canned pineapple rings, drained
    well and chopped
½ small green (bell) pepper, seeded
    and cut into thin strips
75g/3oz mature (sharp)
    Cheddar cheese
salt and ground black pepper

Serves 4 🕙🕙

1 Preheat the oven to 200°C/400°F/ Gas 6. Cut the baguettes in half lengthways and toast the cut sides until crisp and golden.

2 Spread the tomato sauce evenly over the toasted sides of the baguette slices.

3 Cut the ham into strips and place them on the baguettes with the pineapple and green pepper. Season with salt and pepper.

4 Grate the Cheddar and sprinkle it evenly on top. Place the pizzas on a baking sheet and bake for 15–20 minutes, until crisp and golden.

Chunky Cheese Salad

Something you can really sink your teeth into – this salad is choc-a-bloc with vitamins and energy. Serve on large slices of crusty bread.

You will need

¼ small white cabbage, finely chopped
¼ small red cabbage, finely chopped
8 baby carrots, thinly sliced
50g/2oz small mushrooms, cut
   in quarters
115g/4oz cauliflower, cut in
   small florets
1 small courgette (zucchini), grated
10cm/4in piece cucumber, cubed
2 tomatoes, coarsely chopped
50g/2oz sprouted seeds
50g/2oz/½ cup salted peanuts
30ml/2 tbsp sunflower oil
15ml/1 tbsp lemon juice
50g/2oz/½ cup grated cheese
salt and ground black pepper

Serves 4

1 Put all the prepared vegetables and the sprouted seeds in a bowl and mix together well.

Handy hint

You can experiment with many different kinds of sprouted seeds, which all have their own particular flavour. Sunflower, pumpkin, alfalfa and sesame seed sprouts are especially popular. You can buy them in supermarkets and health-food stores.

2 Stir in the peanuts. Drizzle the oil and lemon juice over. Season well and leave to stand for 30 minutes to allow the flavour to develop.

3 Sprinkle grated cheese over just before serving on large slices of crusty bread. Have extra dressing ready, in case anybody wants more.

Ham and Mozzarella Calzone

A calzone is a kind of "inside-out" pizza — the dough is on the outside and the filling on the inside. For a vegetarian version replace the ham with sautéed mushrooms.

You will need

1 pizza dough mix
115g/4oz/½ cup ricotta cheese
30ml/2 tbsp freshly grated
   Parmesan cheese
1 egg yolk
30ml/2 tbsp chopped fresh basil
75g/3oz mozzarella cheese, cut into
   small cubes
75g/3oz cooked ham,
   finely chopped
olive oil, for brushing
salt and ground black pepper

Serves 2 🍴🍴🍴

1 Preheat the oven to 220°C/425°F/ Gas 7. Make the dough according to the packet instructions. Divide it in half and roll out each piece on a floured surface to an 18cm/7in round.

2 Mix together the ricotta and Parmesan cheeses, egg yolk, basil, salt and pepper in a bowl.

3 Spread the mixture over half of each round, leaving a 2.5cm/1in border. Sprinkle the mozzarella and ham on top. Dampen the edges with water and fold over the plain dough.

4 Press the edges to seal. Place on two greased baking sheets. Brush with oil and make a small hole in the top of each for the steam to escape. Bake for 15–20 minutes, until golden.

Roasted Tomato and Pasta Salad

Everybody will love this salad – not just vegetarians. Roasted tomatoes are very juicy, with an intense, smoky-sweet flavour.

2 Bring a pan of lightly salted water to the boil, add the pasta shapes, bring back to the boil and cook for 10–12 minutes, or according to the instructions on the packet.

3 Put the remaining oil in a large bowl with the vinegar, sun-dried tomatoes, sugar and a little salt and pepper to taste. Stir well to mix. Drain the pasta, add it to the bowl of dressing and toss to mix. Add the roasted tomatoes and mix gently.

4 Before serving, add the rocket leaves, toss lightly and taste to see if there is enough salt and pepper. Serve at room temperature or chilled.

You will need

450g/1lb ripe baby Italian plum
  tomatoes, halved lengthways
75ml/5 tbsp extra virgin olive oil
2 garlic cloves, cut into
  thin slivers
225g/8oz/2 cups dried pasta
  shapes, such as shells, butterflies
  or spirals
30ml/2 tbsp balsamic vinegar
2 pieces sun-dried tomato in olive oil,
  drained and chopped
large pinch of sugar
1 handful rocket (arugula), about
  65g/2½oz
salt and ground black pepper

Serves 4 ⊕⊕

1 Preheat the oven to 190°C/375°F/Gas 5. Arrange the halved tomatoes, cut side up, in a roasting pan, drizzle 30ml/2 tbsp of the olive oil over them and sprinkle with the slivers of garlic and salt and pepper to taste. Roast in the oven for about 20 minutes, turning once.

Try this
If you are in a hurry, you can make the salad with halved raw tomatoes instead.

Four Seasons Pizza

This traditional pizza is divided into quarters, each with a different topping to depict the four seasons of the year.

You will need

45ml/3 tbsp olive oil
50g/2oz/scant 1 cup button (white)
  mushrooms, sliced
1 pizza base, about 25–30cm/
  10–12in diameter
175ml/6fl oz/¾ cup ready-made
  tomato sauce
50g/2oz prosciutto
6 pitted black olives, chopped
4 bottled artichoke hearts in
  oil, drained
3 canned anchovy fillets, drained
50g/2oz mozzarella cheese,
  thinly sliced
8 fresh basil leaves, shredded

Serves 2–4 ⓘⓘ

1 Preheat the oven to 220°C/425°F/
Gas 7. Heat 15ml/1 tbsp of the oil
in a frying pan and cook the
mushrooms over a medium heat,
stirring occasionally, until all the juices
have evaporated. Remove the pan
from the heat and leave to cool.

3 Cut the prosciutto into strips and
arrange with the olives on another
section. Thinly slice the artichoke
hearts and arrange over a third
section. Halve the anchovies
lengthways and arrange with the
mozzarella over the fourth section.

4 Sprinkle over the shredded basil.
Drizzle over the remaining olive oil
and season with black pepper. Bake
the pizza for 15–20 minutes, until
crisp and golden and the mozzarella
cheese has melted. Serve immediately,
cut into wedges.

2 Brush the pizza base with half
the remaining olive oil. Spread the
tomato sauce evenly over the base
and mark into four equal sections
with the blade of a knife, but don't
cut through the pizza base. Arrange
the mushrooms over one marked
section of the pizza.

Spiral Pasta Salad

Colourful, tasty and nutritious, this is the ideal pasta salad for a picnic and makes the most of the deliciously sweet cherry tomatoes available during the summer.

You will need

300g/11oz/2¾ cups dried pasta
  shapes, such as spirals
150g/5oz green beans, cut into
  5cm/2in lengths
1 potato, about 150g/5oz, diced into
  small pieces
200g/7oz cherry tomatoes, halved
2 spring onions (scallions), finely
  chopped or 90g/3½oz leek (the
  white part), finely chopped
90g/3½oz Parmesan cheese, diced
  or coarsely shaved
6–8 pitted black olives, cut into rings

For the dressing

90ml/6 tbsp extra virgin olive oil
15ml/1 tbsp balsamic vinegar
15ml/1 tbsp chopped fresh flat
  leaf parsley
salt and ground black pepper

Serves 6 🍴🍴

1 Bring a pan of salted water to the boil, add the pasta, bring back to the boil and cook for 10–12 minutes, or according to the instructions on the packet. Drain, cool by rinsing under cold water, then shake the colander to remove as much water as possible. Leave to drain.

2 Cook the beans and diced potato in a pan of boiling salted water for 5–6 minutes, or until tender. Drain and leave the vegetables to cool.

3 Make the salad dressing. Put all the dressing ingredients in a large serving bowl with salt and pepper to taste and whisk well to mix.

4 Add the cherry tomatoes, spring onions or leek, Parmesan and olive rings to the dressing, then the cold pasta, beans and potato. Toss well to mix. Cover and leave to stand for about 30 minutes. Taste the salad and add a little more salt and pepper, if necessary, before serving.

Margherita Pizza

This classic pizza is simple to prepare. The sweet flavour of sun-ripened tomatoes works wonderfully with the basil and mozzarella cheese.

2 Using a sharp knife, cut the mozzarella into thin slices.

3 Arrange the sliced mozzarella and tomatoes on top of the pizza base.

You will need

1 pizza base, about 25–30cm/
    10–12in diameter
30ml/2 tbsp olive oil
175ml/6fl oz/¾ cup ready-made
    tomato sauce
150g/5oz mozzarella cheese
2 ripe tomatoes, thinly sliced
6–8 fresh basil leaves
30ml/2 tbsp freshly grated Parmesan
    cheese
ground black pepper

Serves 2–3 🍴🍴

1 Preheat the oven to 220°C/425°F/
Gas 7. Brush the pizza base with
15ml/1 tbsp of the oil and then
spread over the tomato sauce.

4 Coarsely tear the basil leaves, add them to the pizza and sprinkle the top with the grated Parmesan. Drizzle over the remaining olive oil and season with black pepper. Bake for 15–20 minutes, until crisp and golden. Serve immediately.

Main Meals

Mozzarella and Tomato Skewers

There's stacks of flavour in layers of oven-baked mozzarella, tomatoes, basil and bread. These colourful kebabs will be popular with both your friends and family.

You will need

12 slices white country bread, each about 1cm/½in thick

45ml/3 tbsp olive oil

225g/8oz mozzarella cheese, cut into 5mm/¼in slices

3 ripe plum tomatoes, cut into 5mm/¼in slices

15g/½oz/½ cup fresh basil leaves, plus extra to garnish

salt and ground black pepper

30ml/2 tbsp chopped fresh flat leaf parsley, to garnish

Serves 4 🍴🍴

1 Preheat the oven to 220°C/425°F/Gas 7. Trim off the crusts from the bread and cut each slice into four equal squares. Arrange them on a baking sheet and brush with half the olive oil. Bake for 3–5 minutes, until all the bread squares are a pale golden colour.

2 Remove the bread squares from the oven and place them on a chopping board with all the other prepared ingredients.

3 Make 16 stacks, each starting with a square of bread, followed by a slice of mozzarella, topped with a slice of tomato and a basil leaf. Sprinkle with salt and pepper, then repeat, ending with a piece of bread. Push a skewer through each stack and place the stacks on the baking sheet.

4 Drizzle with the remaining olive oil and bake for 10–15 minutes, until the cheese begins to melt. Garnish with fresh herbs and serve.

Spicy Spuds

Filled baked potatoes make an excellent and nourishing meal. If you're in a hurry, microwave the potatoes. Corn makes an alternative filling to kidney beans.

You will need

4 medium baking potatoes
olive oil, for brushing

For the filling

425g/15oz can red kidney
  beans, drained
200g/7oz/scant 1 cup soft (farmer's)
  cheese or cream cheese
15–30ml/1–2 tbsp mild chilli sauce
5ml/1 tsp ground cumin

Serves 4 🌶🌶

2 When the potatoes are almost ready, prepare the filling. Heat the beans in a medium pan over a low heat, then stir in the cheese, chilli sauce and cumin.

3 Cut the potatoes open along the score lines and push up the flesh from the base with your fingers (protect your hands). Fill with the chilli bean mixture. Serve immediately.

1 Preheat the oven to 200°C/400°F /Gas 6. Using a sharp knife, score the potatoes with a deep cross and rub them all over with olive oil. Place them directly on the oven shelf and cook for about 1 hour, or until tender. They should feel soft when gently squeezed between thumb and finger.

Handy hint

For speed, you can always cook baked potatoes in the microwave. Prick and score the potatoes, then wrap them in kitchen paper and cook them in the microwave on high for about 12 minutes. The more potatoes that are being cooked, the longer the cooking time will be.

Chilli Cheese Nachos

Viva Mexico! Silence that hungry tummy with a truly spicy snack. Make it as cool or as hot as you like, by adjusting the amount of sliced jalapeño chillies.

You will need

115g/4oz chilli tortilla chips
50g/2oz/½ cup grated
    Cheddar cheese
50g/2oz/½ cup grated Red
    Leicester cheese
50g/2oz pickled green jalapeño
    chillies, sliced

For the dip

30ml/2 tbsp lemon juice
1 avocado, coarsely chopped
1 beefsteak tomato,
    coarsely chopped
salt and ground black pepper

Serves 4 🍴🍴

1 Arrange the tortilla chips in an even layer on a flameproof plate which can be used under the grill (broiler). Sprinkle all the grated cheese over and then sprinkle as many sliced pickled jalapeño chillies as you like over the top.

2 Put the plate under a hot grill and toast until the cheese has melted and browned – keep an eye on the chips to make sure they don't burn.

3 Mix the lemon juice, avocado and tomato together in a bowl. Add salt and pepper to taste and serve with the chips.

Handy hint

Don't make the dip much before your party is due to start because avocado discolours when it is exposed to the air, turning from an attractive shade of pale green to unappetizing brownish grey. (It still tastes fine, however.) The lemon juice in the dip helps to prevent this from happening and, if you need to make the dip ahead of time, cover it tightly with clear film (plastic wrap).

Pancake Parcels

Be adventurous with your pancakes. Don't just stick to lemon and sugar: try this savoury version stuffed with a creamy cheese and ham filling for a real change.

You will need

115g/4oz/1 cup plain
  (all-purpose) flour
1 egg
300ml/½ pint/1 ¼ cups milk
2.5ml/½ tsp salt
25g/1oz/2 tbsp butter
fresh chives, to garnish

For the filling

200g/7oz/scant 1 cup cream cheese
  with chives
90ml/6 tbsp double (heavy) cream
115g/4oz ham, cut in strips
115g/4oz/1 cup grated cheese
15g/½oz/¼ cup fresh breadcrumbs
salt and ground black pepper

Serves 4 🍴🍴🍴

1 To make the pancakes, put the flour, egg, a little of the milk and the salt in a large bowl and beat together with a wooden spoon until smooth. Gradually beat in the rest of the milk with a wooden spoon or a balloon whisk until the batter looks like double (heavy) cream. Add the milk gradually or the batter will be lumpy.

2 Melt a little butter in a medium frying pan and pour in just enough batter to cover the base in a thin layer. Tilt and turn the pan to spread the batter out. Cook gently until set, then turn over with a palette knife or spatula and cook the second side. Slide the pancake out of the pan. Repeat to make three more pancakes. Stack them in a pile on a plate, with a piece of greaseproof (waxed) paper between each one to stop them from sticking together.

3 Preheat the oven to 190°C/ 375°F/Gas 5. Make the filling. Beat together the cream cheese and cream in a bowl. Add the ham and half the grated cheese and season well with salt and pepper. Put a spoonful of the cheese and ham mixture in the centre of a pancake.

4 Fold one side over the mixture and then the other. Fold both ends up as well to make a small parcel. Make three more parcels in the same way. Arrange the parcels on a baking sheet, with the joins underneath. Sprinkle the remaining grated cheese and the breadcrumbs over the parcels and cover them with foil. Cook for 20 minutes. Remove the foil and cook for 10 minutes more, until browned. Tie chives around the parcels.

Tortilla Squares

Adding chopped herbs and a few skinned broad beans to a Spanish omelette makes a very summery dish when cut it into small pieces and served as party snacks.

You will need

45ml/3 tbsp olive oil
2 Spanish (Bermuda) onions, thinly sliced
300g/11oz waxy potatoes, cut into 1cm/½in dice
250g/9oz/1¾ cups shelled broad (fava) beans
5ml/1 tsp chopped fresh thyme or summer savory
6 large (US extra large) eggs
45ml/3 tbsp mixed chopped fresh chives and flat leaf parsley
salt and ground black pepper

Serves 6–8 🍸🍸

1 Heat 30ml/2 tbsp of the oil in a 23cm/9in deep non-stick frying pan. Add the onions and potatoes and stir to coat. Cover and cook gently, stirring frequently, for 20–25 minutes, until the potatoes are cooked and the onions are very soft. Do not let the mixture brown.

2 Meanwhile, cook the beans in boiling salted water for 5 minutes. Drain well and set aside to cool. When the beans are cool enough to handle, peel off the grey outer skins and throw them away. Add the beans to the frying pan, together with the thyme or summer savory and season with salt and pepper to taste. Stir well to mix and then cook for a further 2–3 minutes.

3 Beat the eggs with salt and pepper to taste and the mixed herbs, then pour the mixture over the potatoes and onions and increase the heat slightly. Cook gently until the egg sets and browns underneath, gently pulling the omelette away from the sides of the pan and tilting it to allow the uncooked egg to run underneath.

4 Cover the pan with an upside down plate and invert the tortilla on to it. Add the remaining oil to the pan and heat until hot. Slip the tortilla back into the pan, uncooked side down, and cook for a further 3–5 minutes to allow the second side to brown. Slide the tortilla out on to a plate. Cut into squares and serve warm rather than piping hot.

Shepherd's Pie

This tasty dish is always a popular choice – ideal on a cold day, serve with steamed broccoli or green beans to complete the meal.

You will need

30ml/2 tbsp oil
1 onion, finely chopped
1 carrot, finely chopped
115g/4oz/1⅔ cups
    mushrooms, chopped
500g/1¼lb lean chuck steak,
    minced (ground)
300ml/½ pint/1¼ cups beef stock
    or water
15ml/1 tbsp plain (all-purpose) flour
1 bay leaf
10–15ml/2–3 tsp Worcestershire
    sauce
15ml/1 tbsp tomato purée (paste)
675g/1½lb potatoes, boiled
25g/1oz/2 tbsp butter
45ml/3 tbsp hot milk
15ml/1 tbsp chopped fresh tarragon
salt and ground black pepper

Serves 4 🍴🍴🍴

1 Heat the oil in a pan, add the onion, carrot and mushrooms and cook, stirring occasionally, until browned. Stir the beef into the pan and cook, stirring to break up any lumps, until lightly browned.

2 Blend a few spoonfuls of the stock or water with the flour in a small bowl to make a smooth paste, then stir this mixture into the pan. Stir in the remaining stock or water and bring to a simmer (just below boiling), stirring constantly.

3 Add the bay leaf, Worcestershire sauce and tomato purée, then cover and cook over a very low heat for 1 hour, stirring occasionally. Uncover the pan towards the end of cooking to allow any excess liquid to evaporate, if necessary.

4 Preheat the oven to 190°C/375°F/ Gas 5. Meanwhile, gently heat the cooked potatoes for a couple of minutes, then mash with the butter and hot milk and season to taste with salt and pepper.

5 Add the tarragon and seasoning to the meat, then pour into a pie dish. Cover the meat with an even layer of potato and mark the top with the prongs of a fork. Bake for about 25 minutes, until golden brown.

Terrific Tortilla Triangles

A tortilla is a thick omelette with lots of cooked potatoes in it. It is very popular in Spain, where it is cut in thick wedges like a cake and served with bread.

2 Add the mushrooms to the pan and cook for 2–3 minutes more, stirring often, until they have softened. Add the peas and corn and stir them into the potato mixture.

3 Put the eggs and milk in a bowl. Add the Cajun seasoning and a little salt, if you like, and beat well. Level the top of the vegetables and sprinkle the parsley on top. Pour on the egg mixture and cook over a low heat for 10–15 minutes.

4 Put the pan under a hot grill (broiler) to set the top of the tortilla. Serve hot or cold, cut into wedges.

You will need

30ml/2 tbsp sunflower oil
675g/1½lb potatoes, cut into
　small chunks
1 onion, sliced
115g/4oz/1⅔ cups
　mushrooms, sliced
115g/4oz/1 cup frozen peas, thawed
50g/2oz/⅓ cup frozen corn
　kernels, thawed
4 eggs
150ml/¼ pint/⅔ cup milk
5ml/1 tsp Cajun seasoning (optional)
30ml/2 tbsp chopped fresh parsley
salt (optional)

Serves 4 🍴🍴

1 Heat the oil in a large frying pan, add the potatoes and onion and cook for 3–4 minutes, stirring frequently. Lower the heat, cover the pan and cook gently for 8–10 minutes more, until the potatoes are almost tender and the onion is softened.

Handy hint
Make sure the pan can safely be used under the grill (broiler). Shield wooden or plastic handles with foil.

Individual Toads-in-their-hole

Much more fun than one big toad-in-the-hole. Serve these sausage popovers with home-made onion gravy and peas for a filling meal.

2 Lightly oil eight 10cm/4in non-stick Yorkshire pudding tins (muffin pans) and arrange three sausages in each. Cook in the hot oven for about 10 minutes.

3 Carefully take the tins out of the oven and ladle batter into each tin. Put them back in the oven and cook for 30–40 minutes more, until the batter is risen and browned.

You will need
115g/4oz/1 cup plain (all-purpose) flour
1 egg
300ml/½ pint/1¼ cups milk
45ml/3 tbsp fresh mixed herbs, such as parsley, thyme and chives, coarsely chopped
24 cocktail sausages
salt and ground black pepper

For the onion gravy
15ml/1 tbsp oil
2 onions, sliced
600ml/1 pint/2½ cups stock
15ml/1 tbsp soy sauce
15ml/1 tbsp coarse-grain mustard
30ml/2 tbsp cornflour (cornstarch)
30ml/2 tbsp water

Serves 4 🐷🐷🐷

1 Preheat the oven to 200°C/400°F/Gas 6. Put the flour, egg and a little of the milk in a bowl and beat well with a wooden spoon until combined and smooth. Gradually beat in the rest of the milk to make a batter, using a wooden spoon or a balloon whisk. Season well with salt and pepper and stir in the herbs.

4 Meanwhile, heat the oil in a pan. Cook the onions for 15 minutes, until browned. Add the stock, soy sauce and mustard and bring to the boil. Mix the cornflour and water together in a cup and pour into the gravy. Bring to the boil, stirring. Serve with the "toads".

Handy hint
Use vegetarian sausages for friends who don't eat meat.

Chicken Nibbles

These make a great hot snack for parties. You can have everything, including the dip, prepared in advance, ready to cook when your guests arrive.

You will need

4 skinless chicken breast fillets
175g/6oz/3 cups fresh breadcrumbs
5ml/1 tsp ground coriander
10ml/2 tsp ground paprika
2.5ml/½ tsp ground cumin
45ml/3 tbsp plain (all-purpose) flour
2 eggs, beaten
vegetable oil, for deep-frying
salt and ground black pepper
lemon slices, to garnish
fresh coriander (cilantro) sprigs,
    to garnish

For the dip

300ml/½ pint/1¼ cups Greek
    (US strained plain) yogurt
30ml/2 tbsp lemon juice
60ml/4 tbsp chopped fresh coriander
60ml/4 tbsp chopped fresh parsley

Serves 8 ⑪⑪⑪

1 Divide each chicken portion into two natural fillets. Place them between two sheets of clear film (plastic wrap) and, using a rolling pin, flatten each one to a thickness of 5mm/¼in. Cut into diagonal 2.5cm/1in strips.

2 Mix the breadcrumbs with the spices and seasoning. Toss the chicken fillet strips in the flour, keeping them separate. Dip the fillets into the beaten egg and then coat in the breadcrumb mixture.

3 Thoroughly mix all the ingredients for the dip together and season to taste with salt and pepper. Cover and chill until required.

4 Heat the oil in a heavy pan. It is ready for deep-frying when a piece of bread tossed into the oil sizzles on the surface. Fry the chicken strips, in batches, until golden and crisp. Drain on kitchen paper and keep warm in the oven until all the chicken has been fried. Garnish with lemon slices and sprigs of fresh coriander. Serve with the chilled dip.

Popeye's Pie

Tuck into this layered pie packed full of spinach and delicious Greek feta cheese and you too can have bulging muscles.

You will need

75g/3oz/6 tbsp butter

5ml/1 tsp grated nutmeg

900g/2lb fresh spinach, washed and large stalks removed

115g/4oz/1 cup crumbled feta cheese

50g/2oz/½ cup grated Cheddar cheese

275g/10oz filo pastry sheets

10ml/2 tsp mixed ground cinnamon, nutmeg and black pepper

Serves 4 🍴🍴🍴

1 Melt 25g/1oz/2 tbsp of the butter in a large frying pan, add the nutmeg and the spinach and season well with salt and pepper. Cover and cook for 5 minutes, or until the spinach is tender. Drain well, pressing out as much liquid as possible.

2 Preheat the oven to 160°C/ 325°F/Gas 3. Melt the remaining butter in a small pan. Mix the cheeses together in a bowl and season them with salt and pepper. Unfold the pastry so the sheets are flat. Use one sheet to line part of the base of a small, deep-sided, greased roasting pan. Brush the pastry with melted butter. Keep the remaining filo sheets covered with a damp dishtowel, as they dry out very quickly.

3 Continue to lay pastry sheets across the base and up the sides of the roasting pan, brushing each time with melted butter, until two-thirds of the pastry sheets have been used and the pan is covered. Don't worry if they flop over the top edges – they will be tidied up later after you have added the filling.

4 Mix the cheeses and spinach and spread in the pan. Fold the pastry edges over. Crumple up the remaining sheets of pastry and arrange them on top. Brush with melted butter and sprinkle with the spices. Bake for 45 minutes. Turn the oven up to 200°C/ 400°F/Gas 6. Bake for 15 minutes more and cut into squares to serve.

Chicken Cigars

These small, crispy rolls can be served warm as part of a party buffet, although they are also good as snacks with salad.

You will need
1 × 275g/10oz packet of filo pastry
45ml/3 tbsp olive oil
fresh parsley, to garnish

For the filling
350g/12oz minced (ground) chicken
1 egg, beaten
2.5ml/½ tsp ground cinnamon
2.5ml/½ tsp ground ginger
30ml/2 tbsp raisins
15ml/1 tbsp olive oil
1 small onion, finely chopped
salt and ground black pepper

Serves 4 🐔🐔🐔

1 First, make the filling. Mix together the chicken, egg, cinnamon, ginger and raisins in a bowl and season with salt and pepper. Heat the oil in a large frying pan and cook the onion over a low heat, stirring occasionally, for about 5 minutes, until tender. Leave to cool, then add the mixed ingredients.

2 Preheat the oven to 180°C/350°F/Gas 4. Once the filo pastry packet has been opened, keep the pastry covered at all times with a damp dishtowel, except the piece you are using. Work fast, as the pastry dries out very quickly when exposed to the air. Unravel the pastry and cut it into 10 × 25cm/4 × 10in strips.

3 Take one strip, cover the remainder, brush the strip with a little oil and place a small spoonful of the filling about 1cm/½in from the end.

4 Fold the sides inwards to a width of 5cm/2in and roll into a cigar shape. Place on a greased baking tray and brush with oil. Repeat with the remaining ingredients. Bake for about 20–25 minutes, until golden brown and crisp. Garnish with fresh parsley.

Yellow Bean Chicken

An all-time Chinese favourite made with a ready-made sauce, crunchy cashew nuts and spring onions that you can stir-fry in a few minutes. Serve with boiled rice.

You will need

30ml/2 tbsp groundnut (peanut) oil
75g/3oz/¾ cup salted cashew nuts
4 spring onions (scallions),
   coarsely chopped
450g/1lb boneless, skinless chicken
   breast portions, cut in strips
165g/5½oz jar yellow bean sauce

Serves 4 🍗🍗

Handy hint

Broken cashew nuts, which are cheaper than whole ones, are perfect for this dish. You could also use almonds, if you prefer.

1 Heat 15ml/1 tbsp of the oil in a heavy frying pan and cook the cashew nuts over a low heat, stirring frequently, until browned. This does not take long, so keep an eye on them to prevent them from burning. Lift them out with a slotted spoon and put them to one side.

2 Heat the remaining oil and cook the spring onions and chicken for 5–8 minutes, until the meat is browned all over and cooked.

3 Return the nuts to the pan and pour the jar of sauce into the pan. Stir well and cook gently until hot. Serve immediately.

Try this

If you like fish, you could make this dish with diced monkfish fillet or prawns (shrimp) instead of chicken. Cook the monkfish in the same way as the chicken. If you use raw prawns, cook them in step 2 until they change colour. If you use cooked prawns, add them in step 3 with the nuts and yellow bean sauce, as they need only to heat through and will become tough if overcooked.

Bacon Twists

Making bread is always fun, so try this savoury version and add that extra twist to a birthday breakfast or party snack. Serve with soft cheese and herbs.

You will need

450g/1lb/4 cups strong white
  bread flour
10g/¼oz/4 tsp easy-blend
  (rapid-rise) yeast
2.5ml/½ tsp salt
400ml/14fl oz/1¾ cups
  lukewarm water
12 streaky (fatty) bacon
  rashers (strips)
1 egg, beaten

Makes 12 🍴🍴🍴

1 Put the flour, yeast and salt in a bowl and stir them together. Add a little of the water and mix with a knife. Add the remaining water and use your hands to pull the mixture together to make a sticky dough.

2 Turn the dough on to a lightly floured surface and knead it for 5 minutes, or until the dough is smooth and stretchy. Divide into 12 equal pieces and roll each one into a sausage shape.

3 Lay each bacon rasher on a chopping board and run the back of the knife along its length to stretch it slightly. Wind a rasher of bacon around each dough "sausage".

4 Brush the "sausages" with beaten egg and arrange them on a lightly oiled baking sheet. Leave in a warm place for 30 minutes, or until they have doubled in size. Preheat the oven to 200°C/400°F/Gas 6 and cook the "sausages" for 20–25 minutes, until cooked and browned.

Handy hint
Use the same dough mix to make rolls. Tap their bases – if they sound hollow, they're cooked.

Turkey Surprise Parcels

This looks just like a paper parcel, but there's a special treat inside. Put a parcel on each plate, with new potatoes and green vegetables, and let everyone open their own.

You will need

30ml/2 tbsp chopped fresh parsley
4 turkey breast steaks, weighing
    150–175g/5–6oz each
8 streaky (fatty) bacon
    rashers (strips)
2 spring onions (scallions), cut in
    thin strips
50g/2oz fennel, cut in thin strips
1 carrot, cut in thin strips
1 small celery stick, cut in thin strips
grated rind and juice of 1 lemon
salt and ground black pepper
lemon wedges, to serve

Serves 4 🐟🐟🐟

1 Pat parsley over each turkey steak, then wrap two rashers of bacon around each one. Preheat the oven to 190°C/375°F/Gas 5. Cut four 30cm/12in circles of baking parchment and put a turkey steak just off centre on each one.

2 Arrange the vegetable strips on top of the turkey steaks, sprinkle the lemon rind and juice over and season well with salt and pepper.

Handy hint
Fennel tastes like aniseed, so leave it out if you don't like it.

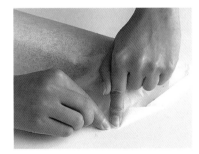

3 Fold the baking parchment over the meat and vegetables and, starting at one side, twist and fold the baking parchment edges together. Carefully work your way around the curve of the semi-circle to seal the edges of the parcel together neatly.

4 Put all four parcels in a roasting pan and cook for 35–45 minutes, or until the meat is cooked and tender. Check that the turkey steaks are cooked right through. Serve the parcels with the lemon wedges to squeeze over them.

Cheese Scrolls

These traditional East European cheese savouries are eaten in cafés, restaurants and homes at any time of the day and are delicious served both warm and cold.

2 Fill a piping (pastry) bag, fitted with a 1cm/½in plain round nozzle, with half the cheese mixture. Fold one sheet of filo pastry into a 30 × 20cm/ 12 × 8in rectangle and brush with a little melted butter. Pipe a strip of feta cheese mixture along one long edge, leaving a margin of about 1cm/½in. Fold in each end to prevent the filling from escaping, then roll up the pastry to form a sausage shape. Brush with more melted butter. Gently twist the "sausage" into an "S" or a crescent shape. Repeat with the remaining ingredients, refilling the piping bag with the feta mixture as necessary.

3 Arrange the filo pastry shapes on a buttered baking sheet and brush with a little more melted butter. Sprinkle with sea salt and chopped spring onions. Bake the pastries for about 20 minutes, until golden brown and crisp. Cool them on a wire rack before serving.

You will need

450g/1lb feta cheese, well drained and finely crumbled
90ml/6 tbsp Greek (US strained plain) yogurt
2 eggs, beaten
14–16 sheets of filo pastry, each measuring 40 × 30cm/16 × 12in, thawed if frozen
225g/8oz/1 cup butter, melted
sea salt and chopped spring onions (scallions), to garnish

Makes 14–16 ⓤⓤⓤ

1 Preheat the oven to 200°C/400°F/ Gas 6. Mix the feta cheese, yogurt and eggs in a large bowl, beating well until the mixture is smooth.

Salmon Fish Cakes

If you like getting your hands very messy, then this is the recipe for you. Serve the fish cakes with green vegetables and buttered new potatoes.

You will need

450g/1lb potatoes, cut in
small chunks
25g/1oz/2 tbsp butter
15ml/1 tbsp milk
425g/15oz can pink salmon, drained,
skinned and boned
1 egg, beaten
60ml/4 tbsp plain (all-purpose) flour
2 spring onions (scallions),
finely chopped
4 sun-dried tomatoes in oil, chopped
grated rind of 1 lemon
vegetable oil, for frying
25g/1oz sesame seeds
salt and ground black pepper

Serves 4 🐟🐟🐟

1 Cook the potatoes in boiling, lightly salted water until tender. Drain and return to the pan. Add the butter and milk and mash well. Season with salt and pepper. Put the mashed potato in a bowl and beat in the salmon. Add the egg, flour, spring onions, tomatoes and lemon rind. Mix well.

2 Share the mixture into eight equal pieces and pat them into fish cake shapes, using floured hands. Put the sesame seeds on a large plate and very gently press both sides of the fish cakes into them, until the cakes are lightly coated.

3 Pour oil into a frying pan to a depth of about 1cm/½in. Heat it gently. Put a small cube of bread in the pan and, if it sizzles, the oil is ready. You may need to cook the fish cakes in several batches. Carefully place the cakes in the pan.

4 When one side is crisp and brown, turn the cakes over carefully with a fish slice to cook the second side. The fish cakes are quite soft and need gentle treatment or they will break up. Lift them out and put them aside to drain on kitchen paper. Keep the cooked fish cakes hot until they are all ready.

Try this
Use canned tuna instead of the salmon, if you like.

Parmesan Thins

These melt-in-the-mouth biscuits are very more-ish, so make plenty. Don't just keep them for parties – they make a great snack at any time of the day.

You will need

50g/2oz/½ cup plain
   (all-purpose) flour
40g/1½oz/3 tbsp butter, softened
1 egg yolk
40g/1½oz/½ cup freshly grated
   Parmesan cheese
pinch each of salt and mustard
   powder

Makes 16–20 🍴🍴

Handy hint

You can freeze the dough in a log shape, wrapped in foil. Thaw for 1 hour before cutting and baking.

1 Rub together the flour and the butter in a large bowl, then work in the egg yolk, grated cheese, salt and mustard powder. Mix well to bring the dough together into a ball. Shape into a log, then wrap in foil or clear film (plastic wrap) and chill for at least 10 minutes.

2 Preheat the oven to 200°C/ 400°F/Gas 6. Cut the dough log into very thin slices, about 3–5mm/ ⅛–¼ in, and arrange them on a baking sheet. Flatten with the back of a fork to give a pretty ridged pattern. Bake for 10 minutes, or until crisp. Cool on a wire rack.

Fish 'n' Rice

This tasty paella-type meal uses a frozen fish mixture that saves lots of preparation time. It is all made in one pan so it saves on washing the dishes too!

You will need

30ml/2 tbsp oil

1 onion, sliced

1 red (bell) pepper, seeded and chopped

115g/4oz/⅔ cup mushrooms, chopped

10ml/2 tsp ground turmeric

225g/8oz/generous 1 cup rice

750ml/1¼ pints/3 cups stock, made with a pilau-rice stock (bouillon) cube

400g/14oz bag frozen shellfish selection, thawed

115g/4oz frozen large tiger prawns (jumbo shrimp), thawed

salt and ground black pepper

Serves 4

2 Stir in the turmeric and then the rice. Stir until thoroughly mixed and the grains of rice are coated with oil, then carefully pour in the stock. Season with salt and pepper, cover with a lid and simmer gently for 15 minutes.

3 Add the shellfish selection and the prawns, stir well and turn up the heat slightly to bring the liquid back to the boil. Cover again and simmer for 15–20 minutes more, until the rice is cooked and tender and the fish is hot. Serve immediately.

1 Heat the oil in a deep frying pan and cook the onion over a medium heat, stirring occasionally, for about 5 minutes, until it is starting to soften. Add the chopped pepper and mushrooms and cook for 1 minute.

Handy hint

If you don't like this fish mixture, choose your own – use more prawns (shrimp), for example, if you prefer, but cut down on the fish cooking time.

Cheese Straws

These will become a family favourite. They are so tasty you may even find them fast disappearing as soon as they have come out of the oven.

You will need

vegetable oil, for greasing
175g/6oz/1½ cups plain (all-purpose) flour
75g/3oz/6 tbsp butter, cut into pieces
115g/4oz/1 cup grated Cheddar cheese
1 egg, beaten

Serves 4–6 👤👤

1 Preheat the oven to 200°C/400°F/ Gas 6. Lightly brush two baking sheets with oil. Place the flour in a bowl and rub in the butter.

2 Stir the grated Cheddar cheese into the flour mixture. Keep 15ml/ 1 tbsp beaten egg on one side for glazing and stir the rest into the mixture. Mix to a smooth dough, adding a little water if necessary.

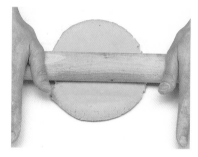

3 Knead lightly, then roll out on a floured surface to a 30 × 20cm/ 12 × 8in rectangle. Brush with the remaining beaten egg.

4 Cut into 7.5 × 1cm/3 × ½in strips and space slightly apart on the baking sheets. Bake the cheese straws for 8–10 minutes, until golden brown. Loosen from, but leave to cool on the baking sheets.

Try this
Spread the cheese pastry with a thin layer of yeast extract for a different version of the straws.

Honey Chops

These tasty sticky chops are very quick and easy to prepare and grill, but they would be just as good cooked on the barbecue. Serve with herbed mashed potatoes or chips.

You will need
450g/1lb carrots
15ml/1 tbsp butter
15ml/1 tbsp soft brown sugar
15ml/1 tbsp sesame seeds

For the chops
4 pork loin chops
50g/2oz/¼ cup butter
30ml/2 tbsp clear honey
15ml/1 tbsp tomato purée (paste)

Serves 4 🐷🐷🐷

Handy hint
If the chops are very thick, increase the time they are under the grill (broiler) to make sure the chops are cooked in the middle.

1 Cut the carrots into thin sticks, put them in a pan and add just enough cold water to cover them. Add the butter and brown sugar and bring to the boil. Turn down the heat and simmer for 15–20 minutes, until most of the liquid has boiled away.

2 Line the grill (broiler) pan with foil and arrange the pork chops on the grill rack.

3 Beat the butter and honey together and gradually beat in the tomato purée to make a smooth paste. Preheat the grill to high.

4 Spread half the honey paste over the chops and grill (broil) them for 5 minutes, until browned.

5 Turn the chops over, spread with the remaining honey paste and return to the grill. Grill for 5 minutes, until the meat is cooked through. Sprinkle the sesame seeds over the carrots and serve with the chops.

Orange and Chive Salsa

Fresh chives and sweet oranges provide a very cheerful combination of flavours and colours. This fruity salsa has a lovely summery feel.

You will need
2 large oranges
1 beefsteak tomato
bunch of chives
1 garlic clove
30ml/2 tbsp olive oil
sea salt

Serves 4 🌶🌶

3 Coarsely chop the orange segments and place them in the bowl with the collected juice. Halve the tomato and use a teaspoon to scoop the seeds into the bowl. Finely dice the flesh and add to the oranges in the bowl.

4 Hold the bunch of chives neatly together and use a pair of kitchen scissors to snip them into the bowl. Thinly slice the garlic and stir it into the orange mixture. Pour over the olive oil, season with sea salt and stir well to mix. Serve within 2 hours.

1 Slice the bottom off the orange so that it will stand firmly on a chopping board. Using a large sharp knife, remove the peel by slicing from the top to the bottom of the orange.

2 Hold the orange in one hand over a bowl. Slice towards the middle of the fruit, to one side of a segment, and then twist the knife to ease the segment away from the membrane and out of the orange. Repeat to remove all the segments. Squeeze any juice from the remaining membrane. Prepare the second orange.

Special Roast Lamb Racks

Racks of lamb are actually lamb chops that are still joined together. They are called "best end" in Britain and "rib chops" in America. Make this as a treat for the whole family.

You will need

2 racks of lamb, with at least four
    chops in each piece
25g/1oz/2 tbsp butter
4 spring onions (scallions),
    coarsely chopped
115g/4oz/generous ½ cup
    basmati rice
300ml/½ pint/1¼ cups stock
1 large ripe mango, peeled and
    coarsely chopped
salt and ground black pepper

For the roast potatoes

900g/2lb potatoes, peeled and cut in
    large, even pieces
30ml/2 tbsp oil
15ml/1 tbsp coarse sea salt

Serves 4 👤👤👤

1 Use a sharp knife to cut the meat off the ends of the bones. Remove and throw away the thick, fatty skin and scrape the bones as clean as possible. Chop the trimmings into small pieces and save them for the stuffing. (The butcher can do all this, if you prefer. Tell him that you are cooking a "Guard of Honour".) Interlock the bones like fingers and tie the two sides together with pieces of string tied around each opposite pair of chops. Stand the racks upright in a roasting pan.

2 Melt the butter in a pan, add the spring onions and lamb trimmings and cook until the meat has browned. Add the rice, stir well to coat the grains with butter and pour in the stock. Bring to the boil, lower the heat, put a lid on the pan and simmer for 8–10 minutes, until the rice is tender.

3 Remove from the heat and stir in the mango to taste. Add salt and pepper. Preheat the oven to 190°C/375°F/Gas 5. Put the stuffing in the middle of the chops. Wrap the ends of the bones in a thin strip of foil and put the roasting pan in the oven. Cook for 30 minutes.

4 While the meat is cooking, make deep cuts in the rounded side of each potato and put them in a pan with cold, salted water. Bring to the boil. Drain and arrange around the outside of the meat. Drizzle the oil over, sprinkle with sea salt and return to the oven for 1–1½ hours, until the potatoes are crisp and the meat is cooked and tender.

Tasty Tomato and Tarragon Salsa

Plum tomatoes, garlic, olive oil and balsamic vinegar make a very Mediterranean salsa – it's always a success at barbecue parties.

2 Slip off the skins and finely chop the tomato flesh. Using a sharp knife, crush or finely chop the garlic.

3 Whisk together the olive oil, balsamic vinegar and plenty of salt and pepper. Finely chop the tarragon and stir it into the olive oil mixture.

4 Mix the tomatoes and garlic in a bowl and pour the tarragon dressing over. Leave to infuse (steep) for at least 1 hour before serving at room temperature. Garnish with shredded tarragon leaves.

You will need

8 plum tomatoes
1 small garlic clove
60ml/4 tbsp olive oil
15ml/1 tbsp balsamic vinegar
30ml/2 tbsp chopped fresh tarragon,
   plus extra to garnish
salt and ground black pepper

Serves 4

1 Skewer the tomatoes, one by one, on a metal fork and hold in a gas flame for 1–2 minutes, turning until the skin splits and wrinkles.

Sticky Fingers

You have to like messy food to eat these sticky pieces of roasted chicken and spare ribs, so keep your napkin handy. Juicy tomatoes make a refreshing accompaniment.

2 Preheat the oven to 190°C/ 375°F/Gas 5. Arrange the chicken thighs and spare ribs in a roasting pan. Spoon the sauce evenly over the meat and cook for 30 minutes. Turn the meat over to make sure that it is coated evenly in the sauce.

3 Cook for 45 minutes more, turning the meat several times and spooning the sauce over it each time. The meat should be really browned and sticky.

You will need

30ml/2 tbsp vegetable oil
1 onion, chopped
1 garlic clove, crushed
30ml/2 tbsp tomato purée (paste)
15ml/1 tbsp white wine vinegar
45ml/3 tbsp clear honey
5ml/1 tsp dried mixed herbs
2.5ml/½ tsp chilli powder
150ml/¼ pint/⅔ cup chicken stock
8 chicken thighs
350g/12oz spare ribs

For the potatoes

675g/1½lb potatoes, cubed
30ml/2 tbsp oil
1 large onion, sliced
1 garlic clove, crushed
salt and ground black pepper

Serves 4 🍴🍴

1 Heat the oil in a heavy pan, add the onion and garlic and cook over a medium heat, stirring occasionally, for about 5 minutes, until the onion starts to soften, but not brown. Add the tomato purée, wine vinegar, honey, mixed herbs, chilli powder and chicken stock, stir well and bring to the boil. Lower the heat and simmer gently for about 15–20 minutes, until the sauce has thickened.

4 Meanwhile, put the potatoes in lightly salted water, bring to the boil, then drain well. Heat the oil in a large frying pan. Add the onion and cook over a medium heat, stirring occasionally, for about 8 minutes, until it starts to turn brown. Add the potatoes and garlic and cook for 25–30 minutes, until everything is cooked through, browned and crisp. Serve with the meat.

Hummus

This delicious Middle Eastern dip can be served with raw vegetable sticks or packed into salad-filled pitta bread, but it is best spread thickly on hot toast.

You will need

400g/14oz can chickpeas, drained
2 garlic cloves
30ml/2 tbsp tahini or smooth
   peanut butter
60ml/4 tbsp olive oil
juice of 1 lemon
2.5ml/½ tsp cayenne pepper
15ml/1 tbsp sesame seeds
sea salt

Serves 4 🍴🍴

1 Rinse the chickpeas well and place in a blender or food processor with the garlic and a good pinch of sea salt. Process until very finely chopped.

2 Add the tahini or peanut butter and process until fairly smooth. Very carefully, with the motor still running, gradually pour in the oil and lemon juice.

3 Stir in the cayenne pepper and add a little more salt to taste. If the mixture is too thick, stir in a little cold water to thin it. Transfer the purée to a serving bowl.

4 Heat a small non-stick pan and add the sesame seeds. Cook for 2–3 minutes, shaking the pan, until the seeds are golden. Leave to cool, then sprinkle over the hummus.

Friday Night Pasta

This is a good pasta sauce made from store-cupboard ingredients, apart from the fresh herbs. It works well with other types of pasta, such as spaghetti, too.

You will need

2 × 15g/½oz packets dried porcini
   mushrooms
175ml/6fl oz/¾ cup warm water
30ml/2 tbsp olive oil
2 shallots, finely chopped
2 garlic cloves, crushed
a few fresh marjoram sprigs, leaves
   stripped and finely chopped, plus
   extra to garnish
1 handful fresh flat leaf
   parsley, chopped
25g/1oz/2 tbsp butter, diced
400g/14oz can chopped Italian
   plum tomatoes
400g/14oz/3½ cups dried rigatoni
25g/1oz/⅓ cup grated Parmesan
   cheese, plus extra to serve
salt and ground black pepper

Serves 4–6 🍴🍴

1 Put the dried mushrooms in a bowl, pour in the warm water and soak for 15–20 minutes. Tip into a fine sieve set over a bowl and squeeze the mushrooms to release as much liquid as possible. Set the mushrooms and the strained liquid to one side.

2 Heat the oil in a frying pan and cook the shallots, garlic and herbs for 5 minutes. Add the mushrooms and butter and stir until the butter has melted. Season with salt and pepper.

3 Stir in the tomatoes and the saved liquid from the soaked mushrooms. Bring to the boil, then cover, lower the heat and simmer gently for about 20 minutes, stirring occasionally. Meanwhile, cook the pasta according to the instructions on the packet. It should be "al dente" when done.

4 Taste the sauce and add more salt and pepper if necessary. Drain the pasta, saving some of the cooking water, and tip it into a large, warmed bowl. Add the sauce and the grated Parmesan and toss to mix. Add a little cooking water if you like a runnier sauce. Serve immediately, garnished with marjoram and with more grated Parmesan handed separately.

Try this

For a richer sauce, add a few spoonfuls of double (heavy) cream or mascarpone cheese to the sauce just before serving.

Satay Sauce

There are many versions of this tasty peanut sauce. Spear chunks of cooked chicken with cocktail sticks and arrange around a bowl of warm sauce.

You will need

200ml/7fl oz/scant 1 cup
coconut cream
60ml/4 tbsp crunchy
peanut butter
5ml/1 tsp Worcestershire sauce
red Tabasco sauce,
to taste
fresh coconut, to
garnish (optional)

Serves 4

1 Pour the coconut cream into a small pan and heat it gently over a low heat for about 2 minutes.

2 Add the peanut butter and stir vigorously until it is thoroughly blended into the coconut cream. Continue to heat until the mixture is warm, but not boiling.

3 Add the Worcestershire sauce and a dash of Tabasco to taste. Pour into a serving bowl.

4 Use a vegetable peeler to shave very thin strips from a piece of fresh coconut, if using. Sprinkle the coconut over the sauce to garnish and serve immediately.

Macaroni Cheese with Mushrooms

Here's a fancier version of an all-time classic, with mushrooms and pine nuts. Serve with garlic bread and a green salad for a quick and easy meal.

You will need

450g/1lb/4 cups quick-cooking short-cut macaroni

45ml/3 tbsp olive oil

225g/8oz/generous 3 cups button (white) mushrooms, sliced

2 fresh thyme sprigs

25g/1oz/¼ cup plain (all-purpose) flour

1 vegetable stock (bouillon) cube

600ml/1 pint/2½ cups milk

2.5ml/½ tsp celery salt

175g/6oz/1½ cups grated Cheddar cheese

5ml/1 tsp Dijon mustard (optional)

25g/1oz/⅓ cup freshly grated Parmesan cheese

25g/1oz/⅓ cup pine nuts

Serves 4 🍴🍴

1 Bring a pan of salted water to the boil. Add the macaroni and cook according to the packet instructions.

Handy hint

Gratin dishes are flameproof dishes and are usually made of enamel-coated cast iron or porcelain.

2 Heat the oil in a heavy pan. Add the mushrooms and thyme. Cover and cook over a gentle heat for 2–3 minutes. Stir in the flour, crumble in the stock cube and stir constantly until evenly blended. Pour in the milk, a little at a time, stirring after each addition. Add the celery salt and Cheddar cheese. Stir in the mustard, if using, then simmer the sauce briefly for 1–2 minutes, until thickened.

3 Preheat the grill (broiler). Drain the macaroni well, toss into the sauce and share among four individual gratin dishes or pour into one large gratin dish. Sprinkle with the grated Parmesan cheese and pine nuts, then grill (broil) until brown and bubbly. Serve immediately.

Mango and Radish Salsa

The sweet flavour and wonderfully juicy texture of mango in this salsa makes a great contrast with the hot and crunchy radishes.

You will need

1 large, ripe mango
12 radishes
juice of 1 lemon
45ml/3 tbsp olive oil
red Tabasco sauce, to taste
45ml/3 tbsp chopped fresh
   coriander (cilantro)
5ml/1 tsp pink peppercorns
salt

To serve

lettuce leaves
watercress sprigs
slices of seeded bread

Serves 4 🐟

1 Holding the mango upright on a chopping board, use a large knife to slice the flesh away from either side of the large flat stone (pit) in two pieces. Using a smaller knife, carefully trim away any flesh still clinging to the top and bottom of the stone.

2 Score the flesh of the mango halves deeply, taking care to avoid cutting through the skin: make parallel cuts about 1cm/½in apart, then turn and cut lines in the opposite direction. Carefully turn the skin inside out so the flesh stands out like hedgehog (porcupine) spikes. Slice the diced flesh away from the skin.

3 Trim the radishes, discarding the root tails and leaves. Coarsely grate the radishes or dice them finely and place in a bowl with the mango cubes. Combine the lemon juice and olive oil with salt and a few drops of Tabasco sauce to taste in a jug (pitcher), then stir in the chopped coriander.

4 Coarsely crush the pink peppercorns in a pestle and mortar or place them on a chopping board and flatten them with the heel of a heavy-bladed knife. Stir into the lemon oil. Toss the radishes and mango, pour in the dressing and toss again. Chill for up to 2 hours before serving.

Vegetarian Tomato Pasta

The riper the tomatoes, the better their flavour. Use only very red plum tomatoes or giant beefsteaks to make this simple and delicious pasta.

You will need

675g/1½lb ripe Italian plum
  tomatoes or beefsteak tomatoes
60ml/4 tbsp extra virgin olive oil or
  sunflower oil
1 onion, finely chopped
350g/12oz fresh or dried spaghetti
a small handful fresh basil leaves
salt and ground black pepper
coarsely shaved Parmesan cheese,
  to serve

Serves 4 🍴🍴

1 With a sharp knife, cut a cross in the base end of each tomato. Plunge the tomatoes, a few at a time, into a bowl of boiling water. Leave for 30 seconds or so, then lift them out with a slotted spoon and gently drop them into a bowl of cold water. Drain well. The skin will have begun to peel back from the crosses. Remove it entirely and throw it away. Place the tomatoes on a chopping board and cut into quarters, then eighths and chop as finely as possible.

Handy hint

The Italian plum tomatoes called San Marzano are the best variety to use. When fully ripe, they have thin skins that peel off easily.

2 Heat the olive or sunflower oil in a large pan, add the onion and cook over a low heat, stirring frequently, for about 5 minutes, until softened and lightly coloured. Add the tomatoes, season with salt and pepper to taste, bring to a simmer, then turn the heat down to low and cover the pan with a lid. Cook, stirring occasionally, for 30–40 minutes, until the mixture is thick and pulpy.

3 Meanwhile, cook the pasta according to the instructions on the packet. Shred the basil leaves finely, or tear them into small pieces.

4 Remove the sauce from the heat and stir in the basil. Drain the pasta, then tip it into a warmed bowl, pour the sauce over and toss well. Serve immediately, with shaved Parmesan in a separate bowl.

Party
Food

Spaghetti with Meatballs

Meatballs simmered in a sweet and spicy tomato sauce are truly delicious with spaghetti. Leave out the chillies if you don't like spicy food.

You will need

350g/12oz minced (ground) beef
1 egg
60ml/4 tbsp coarsely chopped fresh
    flat leaf parsley
2.5ml/½ tsp crushed dried
    red chillies
1 thick slice white bread,
    crusts removed
30ml/2 tbsp milk
about 30ml/2 tbsp olive oil
300ml/½ pint/1¼ cups passata
    (bottled strained tomatoes)
400ml/14fl oz/1⅔ cups
    vegetable stock
5ml/1 tsp granulated sugar
350–450g/12oz–1lb fresh or
    dried spaghetti
salt and ground black pepper
freshly grated Parmesan cheese,
    to serve

Serves 6–8 🍲🍲🍲

1 Put the beef in a large bowl. Add the egg, half the parsley and half the crushed chillies (if using). Season well with salt and pepper. Tear the bread into small pieces and place in a small bowl. Moisten with the milk. Leave to soak for a few minutes,

2 Squeeze out the excess milk and crumble the bread over the meat mixture. Mix everything together with a wooden spoon. Squeeze and knead the mixture until it is smooth.

3 Rinse your hands in cold water, then roll small pieces of the mixture between your palms to make about 40–60 small balls. Place the meatballs on a tray and chill in the refrigerator for about 30 minutes.

4 Heat the oil in a non-stick frying pan. Cook the meatballs, in batches, until browned on all sides. Gently heat the passata and stock in a large pan, then add the remaining chillies (if using) and the sugar, with salt and pepper to taste. Add the meatballs, then bring to the boil. Lower the heat, cover and simmer for 20 minutes.

5 Cook the pasta according to the packet instructions. Drain and tip it into a large, warmed bowl. Pour the sauce over it and toss gently. Sprinkle with the remaining parsley and serve with grated Parmesan.

Gondolier's Risotto

A classic risotto from the Veneto region of Italy where gondolas are used to transport passengers. It is served as a first course in Italy, but it also makes an excellent lunch.

You will need

75g/3oz/6 tbsp butter
1 small onion, finely chopped
275g/10oz/1½ cups risotto rice
about 1.75 litres/3 pints/7½ cups
   boiling chicken stock
225g/8oz/2 cups frozen petits pois
   (baby peas), thawed
115g/4oz cooked ham, diced
salt and ground black pepper
50g/2oz Parmesan cheese,
   to serve

Serves 4 🍴🍴🍴

3 Cook, stirring constantly, until the stock has been absorbed. Add the remaining stock, a little at a time, stirring constantly. Add the peas towards the end. The rice should be tender and the risotto moist and creamy after 20–25 minutes.

4 Gently stir in the ham and the remaining butter. Heat until the butter has melted, then taste to see if more salt and pepper are needed. Transfer to a warmed serving bowl. Grate or shave a little Parmesan cheese over the top.

1 Melt 50g/2oz/4 tbsp of the butter in a pan. Add the onion and cook gently for about 3 minutes, stirring frequently, until softened.

2 Add the risotto rice to the pan. Stir for 1 minute, then pour in a little of the hot chicken stock, with salt and ground black pepper to taste.

Pepperoni Pasta

Spicy pepperoni sausage adds extra zip to any pasta dish — here it is combined with sweet red onion and pesto — a basil and pine nut sauce.

You will need

275g/10oz/2½ cups dried pasta
175g/6oz pepperoni sausage, sliced
1 small or ½ large red onion, sliced
45ml/3 tbsp green pesto
150ml/¼ pint/⅔ cup double (heavy) cream
225g/8oz cherry tomatoes, halved
15g/½oz fresh chives
salt

Serves 4 🍲🍲

1 Cook the pasta in a pan of lightly salted, boiling water, according to the instructions on the packet.

2 Meanwhile, gently cook the sausage slices and the onion together in a frying pan until the onion is soft. The oil from the sausage will mean you won't need extra oil.

3 Mix the pesto sauce and cream in a jug (pitcher). Add to the frying pan and stir until the sauce is smooth. Add the cherry tomatoes and snip the chives over the top with scissors.

4 Drain the pasta and tip it back into the pan. Pour the sauce over and mix well, making sure all the pasta is coated. Serve immediately.

Handy hint

Penne pasta, shaped like quill pens, is a good choice for this dish. Serve with sesame bread sticks for an extra treat.

Try this

Use a mixture of red and yellow cherry tomatoes for a really colourful meal.

Mexican Rice

Versions of this dish are popular in Mexico and all over South America. It is a delicious medley of rice, tomatoes and aromatic flavourings.

2 Heat the oil in a large, heavy pan, add the rice and cook over a medium heat until it becomes a delicate golden brown. Stir the rice occasionally to prevent it from sticking to the base of the pan.

3 Add the tomato mixture and stir over a medium heat until all the liquid has been absorbed. Stir in the chicken stock, salt, whole chilli, if using, and peas, if using. Continue to cook the mixture, stirring occasionally, until all the liquid has been absorbed and the rice is just tender.

You will need

200g/7oz/1 cup long grain rice
200g/7oz can chopped tomatoes in tomato juice
½ onion, coarsely chopped
2 garlic cloves, coarsely chopped
30ml/2 tbsp vegetable oil
450ml/¾ pint/scant 2 cups chicken stock
2.5ml/½ tsp salt
1 fresh green chilli (optional)
150g/5oz/1¼ cups frozen peas (optional)
ground black pepper

Serves 6 🍶🍶

1 Put the rice in a large, heatproof bowl and pour over boiling water to cover. Stir once, then leave to stand for 10 minutes. Tip into a strainer over the sink, rinse under cold water, then drain again. Set aside to dry slightly. Meanwhile, pour the tomatoes and their can juice into a food processor, add the onion and garlic and process until smooth.

Try this

Instead of using peas, add some green (bell) peppers.

4 Remove the pan from the heat, cover it with a tight-fitting lid and leave it to stand in a warm place for 5–10 minutes. Remove the chilli, if using, fluff up the rice lightly with a fork and serve, sprinkled with black pepper. The chilli may be used as a garnish, if you like.

Vegetable Paella

A delicious, tasty all-in-one pan meal that is bound to be a sure-fire hit among vegetarians and meat-eaters alike.

You will need

1 onion, chopped
2 garlic cloves, crushed
2 leeks, sliced
3 celery sticks, chopped
1 red (bell) pepper, seeded
    and sliced
2 courgettes (zucchini), sliced
175g/6oz/2½ cups brown cap
    (cremini) mushrooms, sliced
175g/6oz/1½ cups frozen peas
450g/1lb/2 cups long grain
    brown rice
400g/14oz can cannellini
    beans, drained
900ml/1½ pints/3¾ cups
    vegetable stock
few saffron threads
225g/8oz/2 cups cherry tomatoes
45–60ml/3–4 tbsp chopped fresh
    mixed herbs

Serves 6

1 Put the onion, garlic, leeks, celery, pepper, courgettes and mushrooms in a large pan and mix together.

2 Add the peas, brown rice cannellini beans, vegetable stock and saffron threads to the pan and mix well.

Handy hint

Saffron comes from a kind of crocus and it takes up to 250,000 flowers to produce 450g/1lb of the spice – no wonder it is the most expensive spice in the world.

3 Bring to the boil, stirring, then lower the heat and simmer, uncovered, stirring occasionally, for about 35 minutes, until almost all the liquid has been absorbed and the rice is cooked and tender.

4 Halve the cherry tomatoes and stir them in, together with the chopped herbs. Serve immediately, garnished with lemon wedges and celery leaves.

Chicken Paella

There are many variations of this basic Spanish recipe. Any seasonal vegetables can be added, as can mussels and other shellfish. Serve straight from the pan.

You will need

4 chicken legs (thighs and
  drumsticks)
60ml/4 tbsp olive oil
1 large onion, finely chopped
1 garlic clove, crushed
5ml/1 tsp ground turmeric
115g/4oz chorizo sausage or
  smoked ham
225g/8oz/generous 1 cup long
  grain rice
600ml/1 pint/2½ cups chicken stock
4 tomatoes, peeled and chopped
1 red (bell) pepper, seeded
  and sliced
115g/4oz/1 cup frozen peas
salt and ground black pepper

Serves 4 ☺☺☺

1 Preheat the oven to 180°C/350°F/
Gas 4. Cut the chicken legs in half.

2 Heat the olive oil in a 30cm/12in
paella pan or large flameproof
casserole and brown the chicken
pieces on both sides. Add the onion
and garlic and stir in the turmeric.
Cook for 2 minutes.

Handy hint
Chorizo is a spicy Spanish
sausage that can be very hot.

3 Slice the chorizo sausage or dice
the ham and add to the pan with
the rice and chicken stock. Bring to
the boil over a medium heat and
season to taste with salt and pepper.
Cover and bake for 15 minutes.

4 Remove and add the chopped
tomatoes, sliced red pepper and
frozen peas. Return to the oven and
cook for a further 10–15 minutes, or
until the chicken is tender and the rice
has absorbed the stock.